The DIARY of a TEENAGE GIRL

AN ACCOUNT
IN WORDS AND PICTURES

· PRAISE *for* THIS BOOK ·

❝ Intensity, thy name is Gloeckner. This 2002 novel, about a young woman's often-traumatic coming of age in 1970s San Francisco, is a complicated combination of standard written-through passages, comic strips and illustrations; it's about as far you can go into the realm of the novel without entirely relying on prose. Is it autobiography? Is it fiction? Either way, it is a tough, necessary read.❞
—*Rolling Stone*

❝ The book inspires a powerfully ambivalent feeling—half disgust and half sympathy—which may be the point. As Gloeckner seems to hint in her dedication, there's likely a piece of the immature, naive, and damaged Minnie in most teenage girls, and *Diary* allows readers to explore that awkward time without moralistic judgment ... Gloeckner, regarded as one of the best American underground female comic artists, has never been afraid to raise a ruckus, yet as titillating and voyeuristic as *Diary* can be (and intends to be), it's Minnie's search for self-love that makes the book compelling.❞
—Bernice Yeung, *SF Weekly*

❝ What's unusual and wonderful about Gloeckner's writing and art is its unflinching engagement with messy truths. *The Diary of a Teenage Girl* is shockingly—and refreshingly—frank, strongly conveying what it's like to be a sexual girl in a problematic world.❞
—Chris Dodge, *Utne Reader*

MORE PRAISE *for* THIS BOOK

" [*Diary* displays] ... a kindred range of perception regarding the data and colorings of a teenaged sphere; an accommodation both robust and delicate for teenage language, with a shrewd recognition of its diverse cultural influences; and a warm comprehension of the combined recklessness, cluelessness, and gallantry attending a young girl/woman's encounter with horrendous moral squalor: not only the promiscuities and dissipations of the street; but those masked or camouflaged within and by the home."
—*The Comics Journal*

" Gloeckner has become an admirable cartoonist not only for the power of her work, and not solely for her continued grasp of comics narrative, but for the way in which her comics have fallen in tune with her moral outlook. Gloeckner's best stories regard truth as an unattainable goal but perhaps the only one worth pursuing. Her art may be the closest approximation of our own silent recalibrations and reconfigurations, our attempts to do justice to the past while making our way in the present. As the artist herself puts it, "The truth always changes, and in the end there is almost no truth.""
—*The Comics Reporter*

" The Minnie stories describe an adolescence that is at once traumatic and picaresque. They explore the power a girl feels in her emerging sexuality as well as the damage inflicted by those who prey upon it. In the process, they raise unsettling questions about vulnerability, desire and the nature of a young woman's victimization ... Gloeckner is arguably the brightest light among a small cadre of semiautobiographical cartoonists"
—Peggy Orenstein, *New York Times*

" Brave and voyeuristic, *Diary* is an exercise in genre-bending. It defies critical classification: call it proto-feminist biography, post-modern memoir, meta-narrative or coming-of-age smut, but its fans are many and varied."
—Nathalie Atkinson, *Broken Pencil*

" With *Diary*, Gloeckner has essentially created her own medium."
—Sari Globerman, *Bust* **magazine**

" Phoebe Gloeckner is a great artist."
—R. Crumb

but I do...
he won't t...
just as easily he doesn't...
just gets so depressed and it j... is so... he w...
t even know what kind of relationship...
they all just expect me to know. It was just the same with
ative sometimes. It was just the same with
ding information out of me about my mother and then telling...
ss I could tell her for him I hate it I hate it and
e of it has anything to do with me. I am not goingvto tell my
ther what   told me to know so badly let them settle it between
o him and she wants to know so badly let them settle it between
each other. It's so depressing no one as ever happy someone is always disgusted or depressed.   Yuk Yuk Yuk Yuk Yuk
I refuse to let myself be drawn into to such things which do not
rightly concern me.

I was awful last night I had alot of alchoholic beverages at a bar the bar is
what got me started.I hate places like that. All the women are trying to look
sexy and are only sueceeding at looking dryed up and boring and the men all try
to look masculi...   tight silk shirts etc. so that they can attract these boring
dryed up wom...   person in the establishment obviously-I shouldn't
have been t...   ...n't think of any reason at all to drink unless
you go all   ...and scream and... stumble all over
the place.   ...drinking"...occupy... the point?
Maybe you   ...while your'e
waiting to   ...you do.
Anyway The   ...ughing and
staring a...   ...e so many men
the eye y...   ...out their chests
trying t...   ...ad seven rum an
d grape...   drinks as little
(i mean...   te strange(unenjoy-
able? g...   pastimes of the olde
general...ight.   ...as I journeyed throu
the sta... convince

to his apartment so
I had to ...quite remember   ...ery unclear.....the
we did I can't quite remember   ...then,and the poisone
liquor had been completely absorb...I wa...somehow so it will loose some o...
liqid had enveloped my brain....I wa... drunk   ...The strange thing i
would not beleive that I was   ...ng,in his eyes,natu...
when I use that term,so I have to screw it up   ...I get really embarra...
intensity) I refused to put my clothes back on. I threatened to simply walk o...
door and up and down the hallway completely nude.   was furious. He yelled and
And told me he'd kill me and I told him to get his stinking hands off of me
tell my mother....then he left me alone and swearing under his breath,w...
his stuffy little kitchenette and had about half a big hunkin loaf of lima
bread.   I was still naked and not embarrasssed in the least and demanded
sssss or a piece of bread because if I didn't get what I wanted,I would
undressed. Then he got really really mad and yelled at the top of his lu
would never have anything to do with me again and that the whole thing h

think I
ore.....but he
...ot related. It's di
...ationship mingle in my
...l as I like him it's in a
ne way I do.....but I souldn't ex
difficult it is to be alone with my grandparent... because
way out.......she said she'd take me... to lov
my mother is so sweet. But I need somebody to lov
dsy I wanted to as soon as they left. to the beach an
what if I ever getreally close to her and we talk about
ything else....then I'll want to tell her about
if I don't I feel incompletely with her and kind of gui
if she thinks she knows everything
things you just can't tell   I know it would
uld really kill her. She'd just thi... but th...
ally a pity I wish I would
like her that I...
d It'...

This book belongs to:

alt...
t v...
e so...
thro...
njoy...
longst...
o...
th the f...
men is empress
everywhere."

The Diary of a Teenage Girl

by Phoebe Gloeckner

 NORTH ATLANTIC BOOKS, BERKELEY, CA

Published by
North Atlantic Books
Berkeley, California

Cover art by Phoebe Gloeckner
Cover and book design by Phoebe Gloeckner and Carl Greene
Printed in the United States of America

The Diary of a Teenage Girl, Revised Edition is sponsored and published by the Society for the Study of Native Arts and Sciences (dba North Atlantic Books), an educational nonprofit based in Berkeley, California, that collaborates with partners to develop cross-cultural perspectives, nurture holistic views of art, science, the humanities, and healing, and seed personal and global transformation by publishing work on the relationship of body, spirit, and nature.

North Atlantic Books' publications are available through most bookstores. For further information, visit our website at www.northatlanticbooks.com or call 800-733-3000.

Nota Bene:
This account is entirely fictional and if you think you recognize any of the characters as an actual person, living or dead, you are mistaken.

New ISBN for this edition: 978-1-62317-034-9

The Library of Congress has cataloged the first edition as follows:
Gloeckner, Phoebe.
    Diary of a teenage girl: an account in words and pictures /
    Phoebe Gloeckner.
        p. cm.
ISBN 1-58394-080-4 (hardcover)
ISBN 1-58394-063-4 (paperback)
I. Title.
PS3557.L635D5 2002
813'.54—dc21

99-027253

1 2 3 4 5 6 7 UNITED 19 18 17 16 15

Printed on recycled paper

For my daughters,
Audrey Fina Gloeckner-Kalousek
& Persephone Gloeckner-Suits

- and -

for all the girls

when they have grown

Childhood can never die;
Wrecks of the past
float o'er the memory,
Bright to the last.
Many a happy thing,
Many a daisy spring,
floats on time's ceaseless wing,
far, far away.

Childhood can never die,
Never die, never die,
Childhood can never die,
No, never die.

Abby Hutchinson
CA. 1880

Best friends Minnie and Kimmie.

Contents

Foreword

The Diary of a Teenage Girl is a book unlike any other you will read; it has no comparison or competitor. It weights the wild exuberance of the young Minnie Goetze, with her keen observing eye, massive vocabulary, and straightforward need to be loved, with the controlled hand of an auteur totally in charge of her craft.

The importance of both of Phoebe Gloeckner's major long-form works, *A Child's Life and Other Stories* (1998) and *The Diary of a Teenage Girl: An Account in Words and Pictures* (first published in 2002), is hard to overstate. In the relatively short thirteen or so years since *Diary of a Teenage Girl* was first published, it has become a classic in the comics field, and for anyone and everyone interested in the experiences of young women. I am thrilled that there is now not just a new edition of Phoebe's seminal novel but also an off-Broadway stage adaptation and a full-length feature film based on this work. People from many different fields have been inspired by the creativity of *Diary*.

The Diary of a Teenage Girl is a totally uninhibited object. The protagonist, Minnie, who lives in San Francisco and starts an affair with her mother's boyfriend when she is only fifteen, keeps an expressive diary that constitutes the large portion of the book. Minnie's complicated sense of her own sexuality (which she both celebrates and derides; her views are decidedly not one-note) and her sexual experiences are chronicled in detail. While it has become commonplace to praise a work for being "raw," I can state truly that *Diary* is probably the "rawest" book I have ever read; I actually had a hard time reading some passages because of how unfiltered they feel, providing a direct line to the alternately wounded and ecstatic teenage psyche. But the kind of discomfort one might feel reading *Diary*—say, about how much a fifteen-year-old loves getting fucked—is an important kind of discomfort. *Diary* stands alone in my mind for its brave, unabashed take on the complexity of life at this age. And this is just in the prose.

Diary is also populated throughout by images rendered in Phoebe's incredibly supple, sensual, detailed hand. In addition to her job as a tenured professor at the Stamps School of Art and Design at the University of Michigan, Phoebe is also a trained medical illustrator, and she is widely acknowledged as one of the finest draftspeople in comics. *Diary,* presenting a dense, realistic style with a twist, offers images that sweetly chronicle the granular and the everyday (maps of the family neighborhood and apartment, illustrations of Minnie's favorite candy, visual inventories of Minnie's room), alongside suggestive and graphic ones of sex and drugs.

Diary's brilliance is in its rich form as a narrative—"an account in words and pictures." Its craftedness counterbalances the uneven, passionate, wildly oscillating and totally unbridled voice of its diarist. Inspired in part by nineteenth-century illustrated novels, such as those by Zola, *Diary* exceeds the form of illustrated novel: it creates entirely its own genre in which images propel the narrative in multivalent ways. The book consistently alternates between prose and images. There are spot illustrations throughout, interrupting the flow of text, and there are also full-page, captioned images (samples: "Ricky Ricky Ricky Wasserman, that exquisitely handsome boy" and "I would like to die by drownation in the Ganges River"); further, and perhaps most significantly, the prose periodically breaks out into comics form for pages at a time, taking over the narrative. These interspersed comics, in picturing and framing Minnie's experience, add to the record the visual voice of the adult author who is interpreting Minnie's experiences for readers. *Diary* is a hybrid and dialogic text—both across its words and images, and in the profound and moving tacit dialogue it stages between different versions of self.

The dedication for *The Diary of a Teenage Girl* reads: "For all the girls when they have grown." I like to think of this as Phoebe dedicating the book, in a sense, to herself, as well as to its many readers.

—HILLARY CHUTE

Associate Professor, Department of English
University of Chicago

Preface to the Revised Edition

I wrote this book with you in mind, and it's for you if you'll have it.

It incorporates, in part, the diary I kept as a teenager. In that sense, I suppose I started writing this book a very long time ago, when I was very young.

What I have always hoped is that the central character, Minnie Goetze, is a person to whom readers will relate, whether they be female, male, old, or young. Minnie is, first and foremost, a human being. That she is female and young are secondary.

The Diary of a Teenage Girl has often been characterized as autobiography, life-writing, or memoir. These characterizations seem to attempt to define the book as a "document," or in "feminist" terms, as a record of a young woman's life in a particular era, a record whose value is more political and historical than aesthetic or literary.

I see my work differently. This book is a novel. The differences between a diary and a novel (even a novel with the word "Diary" in its title) are important to consider.

A diary is a history of thought, event, and emotion whose creation is a consecutive recording of an individual life. It is an artifact and asks for no redaction. A novel, on the other hand, is an encapsulated world created by the author, one that we are invited to enter and believe in, although its reality is artifice.

The question I've most often been asked about this book is, "Is it true? Is it about your own experience?" I am confounded by this question. While a work of "art" should not be confused with its creator, they are, admittedly, inextricable. In many ways, this book is "about" me. However, this book is just as strongly about you, too. I aspire to create characters who can be universally understood despite being constructed with details so numerous that they could only refer to a particular situation. Although I am the source of Minnie, she cannot be me—for the book to have real meaning, she must be all girls, anyone. This is not history or documentary or a confession, and memories will be altered or sacrificed, for factual truth has little significance in the pursuit of emotional truth. It's not my story. It's our story.

Having flogged the dead horse of autobiography, I'd like to respond to frequent descriptions of this book as being about "trauma" or "the sexuality of the female adolescent." Again, all coyness aside, I must tell you that it is "about" nothing. At the same time, it is "about" everything. It is about being born into certain circumstances, and moving, at some point, toward independent action and consciousness of one's own desires, limitations, and capabilities. It's about pain and love. It's about life. That's all.

—PHOEBE GLOECKNER

Associate Professor, Stamps School of Art and Design
University of Michigan, Ann Arbor

THE DIARY OF A TEENAGE GIRL

an account in words and pictures

A Note of Caution to the Reader

Dear Dear,

Please, do never read this unless and until I am dead and even then not unless it is twenty-five years from now or more.

This book contains private information. On these pages I have spilled my feelings and thoughts as they have come to me, spontaneously. I would not care so much if I hadn't written things that are directly connected to the lives of others, but I have, and if you do read this you may be deeply hurt and bewildered and confused and you may even cry, so please, do not read any further.

If you do read on, don't you dare ever let me know that you did or I swear to God I will kill myself or run away or do any number of self-destructive things. I beg of you, for my sake and yours, do not do not do not.

Minnie Goetze
San Francisco, CA

Just like the candy, pronounced "GETZ".

Spring

My introduction to love

———

This book was begun in earnest
on a cold, foggy evening in March 1976
coincidentally
the occasion of a full moon
which could only be seen
from this part of the Earth
through breaches
in the layer of fog.

I don't remember being born.

I DON'T REMEMBER BEING BORN. I was a very ugly child. My appearance has not improved so I suppose it was a lucky break when he was attracted by my youthfulness.

My name is Minnie Goetze.

My body is fairly evenly proportioned. I'm shortish (about 5'4"), with broad shoulders and broad hips and a little waist and my breasts keep growing but they're still not big. I have a squarish face to match my body, with big eyes that are green, a biggish nose that tilts upward, a regular mouth, square teeth, and dark eyebrows.

I live in San Francisco, on Clay Street, in a neighborhood called Laurel Heights, a half-block from the Korean Consulate. It's a rich neighborhood, but we are not rich—I live in an apartment, in the middle flat of three in a Victorian house with my mother and my sister Gretel, who is thirteen.

I'm fifteen years old. I'm in tenth grade.

I like being alone, and I'm not stupid, and I think a lot, and I don't usually talk much unless I know the person well, and then I just can't stop talking unless I'm in a quiet mood which is at least twice a day when I'm with other people and most of the time when I'm with myself only. I am a very physical person. I'm always running around and sometimes I hit people just for pretend. Especially Monroe. We box around all the time. I've been going to bed around midnight lately, and waking up at 9:30. I wash my hair every day. I had it cut last night. It's brown and a few inches past my shoulders.

Drawing and writing are the things I like to do best. I'm also interested in science, and my grandparents want me to become a doctor because my grandmother's one and they think of all the grandchildren, I'm the most likely to follow in her footsteps but I don't want to do that.

For the first half of the school year, I was a student at a boarding school in Palo Alto. I came back only every other weekend. I tired of this, and begged to come home. So here I am. I started going to a new school in January. My sister and I have almost always gone to private schools, but that's because my grandfather pays our tuition. We're usually the poorest kids at school.

We have one pet—a cat named Domino.

Since about two weeks ago, I've developed quite a taste for eggs. I eat an average of four a day, usually more, sometimes less.

———

In all matter-of-factuality, it happened like this:

One night, my mother's boyfriend, Monroe, let me drink some of his wine. We were sitting on the living room couch. My mother and my sister Gretel had gone to sleep. I got drunk and he kept putting his arm around me. "Look at this silly little flannel nightgown," he said. I had on the nightgown Granny gave me at Christmas, with white and blue stripes. "It makes you look like a little girl. But you're fifteen now right Jesus Christ I can't believe it it seems like just yesterday that I met you how old were you then? Eleven or twelve, right? Jesus Christ." He sort of rubbed my breast through my nightgown but I was so surprised by what he was doing that even though I half-felt that it was rude and presumptuous of me to think he was doing this intentionally, I backed away because I didn't want him to feel how small my breasts were, even by accident. I felt I should dismiss the entire incident no matter how I interpreted it—we were both drunk. And I also had this strangely calming feeling that even if he had touched my tits on purpose that it was probably all right because he's one of our best friends and he's a good guy and he knows how it goes and I don't.

A couple of nights later Mom decided she didn't want to go to a nightclub with Monroe (as she had planned) to see some singing cowboys. She said, "Why don't you take Minnie?"

He says, "Well, kid, whadya think? You want to go out on the town with me? Your mom's standing me up!"

"Well, ok...," I said with little enthusiasm. Of course I had homework but so the fuck what. I wanted to go, so I did and of course I was served a drink or two because I am so mature-looking. And Monroe always seems to drink under such circumstances. We were laughing at the fools on the stage and the waitresses told us to stop making such godfucking noise so we went to the back of the room. He was feeling my tits but I kept interrupting him to stumble over to the ladies' room. He was saying, "Oh look you're giving me a hard-on oh look you're givingmeahardon." Then he put

Our building and street.

my hand down his pants but it didn't feel too hard to me. It had soft skin. I don't know what I expected exactly but I guess flesh can never be really hard, like Formica or wood, because it is, after all, flesh. I told him I wanted him to fuck me and he said are you crazyohgodlookyou'regivingmeahardon.

I said I really mean it I really really want you to fuck me. I was laughing and it seemed ridiculous. I didn't even know if I was serious but it was a funny game and I was totally drunk.

"Jesus Christ, Minnie you're shit-faced," he says. "I'm taking you home. Gonna get you back to your goddamn mother." And he pulls me up out of my chair and the waitresses with the stupid-looking faces and blue eye shadow are staring at us like god knows what they're thinking.

We got into his car and we were both very very drunk and he looks at me and says, "I can't believe you want me to fuck you. Do you really want me to fuck you?" "None of your fucking business!" I laughed, and he said, "You really *do* want me to fuck you, don't you? I can't believe it." He tilts his head and squints his eyes in a funny way when he's drunk, and his mouth gets kind of melty and uncontrolled. "You really fuckin' want me to fuckin' fuck you." I laughed again but I wasn't really sure whether I wanted him or anyone else to fuck me but I was afraid to pass up the chance because I might never get another. He started the car and backed out, and we drove towards my house... after a while neither of us said much of anything at all. I had that cold chill gripping my heart and my teeth started chattering like I was freezing or scared.

———

I got so drunk another night that I almost drowned in the bathtub. Mom had been up with us but she fell asleep at 8:00. Monroe let me drink the rest of her wine and more. After a while, I just had to go to sleep. I felt so sick. He went to my room with me, stumbling all over the dirty laundry and books and junk on the floor. It was very nice and comforting the way he rubbed my back as I threw up over the side of my bed. Monroe was too drunk to clean it but he made me get in the bathtub to get the vomit out of my hair. He filled up the tub but then he left the room out of politeness and respect. I started singing aaahhhhhh that's the way uh huh uh huh I like it uh huh uh huh that's the way. Then he told me to shut up or I'd wake my mom and Gretel. So I closed my eyes and leaned back in the warm water.

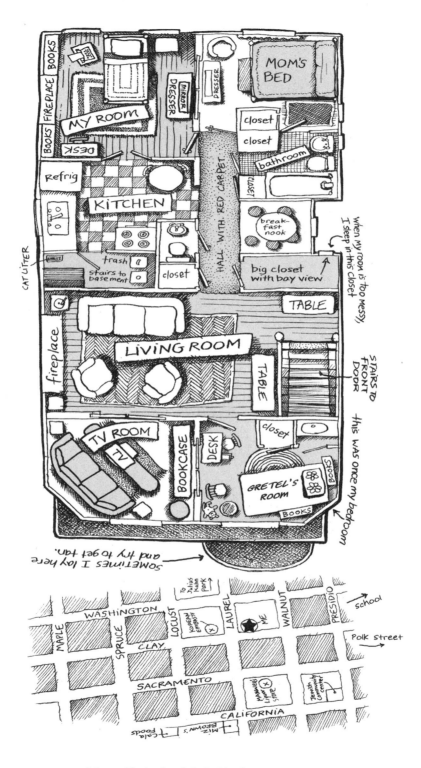

My neighborhood and the inside of our apartment.

My head seemed to spin just like you're told it does when you're drunk. When I got out Monroe was asleep on the couch.

In the morning Mom yelled because I hadn't let the water out of the tub and I left a wet towel on the floor but I told her it wasn't on purpose because I threw up last night. I said I must have the flu, so I didn't go to school. I did feel very sick.

Mom was also home the next night but went to bed after *Mary Hartman Mary Hartman*. It was very romantic the way the black-and-white blueness of the tv light bounced all over the room. He slipped his hand between my legs and then he bent over me and kissed me for a long time. (It tasted like heated wine hot and sticky, the inside of his mouth was all smooth.) Over the course of an hour, before he fell asleep, I tried giving him a blow-job and everything else. He kept saying he wanted to fuck me but he said we can't here.

———

The following Tuesday, I didn't go to school. We had made a plan. I set off at the usual time with my backpack and my books, but I just kept walking right past school and met him at the corner of Jackson and Scott, at the upper left-hand corner of Alta Plaza, if you're looking toward the bay. I suppose he didn't go to work, I don't know, that didn't even occur to me until now.

We drove across the bridge and went to Stinson Beach first and drank beer and ate some sandwiches and watched two wet black dogs fighting over a stick in the sand. Monroe loves the water. Then we went back to San Francisco, to his place in Russian Hill. It hurt and it still hurts and I'm sure it was the most colorful blood that will ever come out of me. Afterwards, we lay quietly beside one another on the bed. We both still had our jackets on, naked from just the waist down. I drew an "X" on his leg with my blood. He said he couldn't believe I was a virgin.

He dropped me off a few blocks from home so no one would see us. As soon as I got inside my mother said, *"Make the frozen peas—it's almost dinner time! Where were you?"* I stood by the stove stirring the peas but I felt blood trickling so I ran to the bathroom and the blood was just everywhere, dripping into the toilet. I didn't know what to do so I just sat there and after a while my mother yelled, "Jesus, the peas are burned! *Minnie, where are you?!"*

I shouted, *"I'm in the bathroom and I can't come out I feel really sick I have diarrhea."* Then she left me alone.

That was a couple of weeks ago, on March 2, to be exact.

I think I've explained enough. I'm going to continue this diary with the intention of writing each and every day, writing as honestly and sincerely as is possible for me to do.

Essential French vocabulary.

Monroe Rutherford is the handsomest man in the world.

Monroe Rutherford is the handsomest man in the world. He is blond and blue-eyed and very tall and strong and he has two big strong muscular thighs and a big hairy chest. He's here all the time, for dinner, or just to hang out. He says we feel like real family to him.

When he's joking, he calls himself a man's man, a businessman, but a mariner at heart, a free spirit.

As for myself, well, I am not particularly attractive at all. I suppose it was my youth, or maybe it has something to do with my mother. He's fucked me three times now and I feel as if I'm being taken advantage of because I know he only loves her....

But whatever the nature of his attraction, I know it has nothing to do with who I really am. For this I do not complain. I'm not exactly in love with him either, you know. I just wish he hadn't all of a sudden decided to feel guilty about what we were doing without thinking about how unguilty I feel about the whole thing. I was just beginning to really like the feeling and now I'm so fucking randy... I don't know where to direct all my sexual energies.

On Saturday, I went to Golden Gate Park, to the aquarium, and picked up this really cute little number only sixteen years old and he had the bluest big eyes and the thickest waviest blond hair and baby lips... his body was like Monroe's but younger, with no fat on it. I had been walking around the dark, u-shaped hall that's lined with fish tanks on either side. I was standing in front of the tank with the alligator gar and the giant sea bass when he came up behind me and said hi.

He made some small talk about fish and then he started walking with me and he put his arm around my waist, but lightly, as if I was his girlfriend.

...the giant sea bass...

He was very handsome and I needed no persuading and it drives me crazy trying to remember his face because I know I'll never see him again. He had a hard-on the minute I took his hand. He gave me big, long, sloppy wet kisses in the dark of the fish museum and I kept squeezing his big huge throbbing cock through his rough corduroy pants and he had his hands up my shirt and everywhere else. After a while we noticed some black guy staring at us and following us so we had to go and find a secret bush outside. The boy had his hands down my pants and I sucked his dick and he wanted to fuck but I couldn't let him do it right there in the park. He rolled on top of me and made all the motions just the same. I could feel how big and hard he was and I really wanted to fuck but I just couldn't. I would just feel too exposed. So then I just rubbed it until he came all over his brand-new grass-green shirt. He was so polite he even brushed off my ass when I stood up. It was awkward. I tried to shake his hand and he tried to kiss me and we said goodbye as if we'd see each other again.

I think his name was Kirk or Kurt. Maybe it wasn't the sexiest thing in the world but it got me off, for a while, at least.

TUESDAY, MARCH 16

I'm not going to destroy this diary. The last one I soaked in the bathtub until the ink ran and the paper got all wet and doughy. Then I rolled the pages up into balls, like the ones you can make with white bread, and I flushed them down the toilet.

That was eighth grade and I was in love with Sarah S—. We used to chase each other around the halls at Hamlin School for Girls and grapple with each other. I remember trying to accidentally rub my chest against hers—we wore white cotton midi blouses and neither of us wore a bra. Just brushing against her arm would give me shivers. We both loved Janis Joplin. I remember Sarah staring into my eyes and saying, "Tell me something deep." I wanted to tell her something, everything, but there was always something more, something I couldn't express, I loved her so much that I was crazy, and I wanted, so many times, to kiss her, so much that I felt faint or close to tears when I looked at any part of her body—her wavy, coarse blond hair, the sharp kneecap above the navy-blue uniform socks, her deep-set blue eyes and priggish mouth. I never questioned whether she was beautiful. There was nothing more satisfactory than thinking of her. I liked to imagine Sarah in a dreadful accident, falling off the roof of the school while she was playing basketball. I would run down the cement stairs to the landing where she lay bleeding and hold her in my arms and kiss her and tell her I loved her. Then she would die, but not before responding to my kiss with a breathless last remark, "Oh, I love you too, how I love you– I have always loved you."

One night I had a dream that my stepfather found the diary, and I woke up full of fear at 3:00 am and destroyed the little book. In the morning I was so sad and regretful that I felt as though my soul had escaped my body and my love for Sarah had been stolen.

We were thirteen then.

LATER

I got a letter today from my stepfather, Pascal:

Dear Minnie,

Did you know that most terrestrial water is seawater (97 percent, 97 out of 100 parts, in other words)? We live on the other 3 percent. Not much drinking water comes out of that either. Of the 3 percent non-sea water the icecaps hold 2 percent (melting ice from the north). The amount of water that cycles each year is one part in 3,000 of the total, most of which falls back into the sea. The amount of water flowing in all the streams is only a couple of weeks' worth of rainfall on land. Lakes hold a three-year supply. Underground water, about which little is known, is perhaps comparable in quantity to the store held as ice (up north, down south).

I am sending you a book on water.

Love,
Pascal

Pascal MacCorkill is an editor of scientific journals and books and he wants me to be interested in science.

I've known Pascal since I was four years old. He lived with us in Philadelphia for several years before he married my mother. We moved to San Francisco three or four years ago because of his job. He and Mom split up very shortly after that. They are now almost divorced. He despises Monroe.

Me and my sister Gretel.

He thinks people who know nothing of math and science are doomed idiots. He is from Scotland and describes his parents as ignorant peasants who live in a thatch-roofed cottage with no central heat or water. They are crude and mean and he hates them and says that ignorance is a most fearsome thing and is to be avoided at all costs.

My real Dad still lives in Philadelphia, but even when I lived there, I didn't see him much, only once or twice a year. He's an artist, but my grandfather supports him, and he likes to party, so he doesn't do much work.

A picture my Dad drew a long time ago.

WEDNESDAY, MARCH 17

It's St. Patrick's Day. Mom and Monroe are out with their friends drinking green beer at the Abbey Tavern on Geary.

Gretel made a Hungry Man Salisbury steak tv dinner and took the tv in her room. She's watching re-runs of The Six-Million-Dollar Man.

Sometimes I feel incapable of love. I have a little feeling that I'm doing something wrong. I can't look at myself objectively. I want someone to say, "Minnie, you shouldn't do that," even though I know it's my business and no one else is interested. I want someone to care enough to say more than just "It's up to you what you do with your life." I don't have any opinions and I don't trust myself.

THURSDAY, MARCH 18

Dear Me,

Some things are too complicated to type down on paper. You just would not understand them even if they were described in the most meticulous detail possible. It is quite difficult to bring these things into focus—even the most powerful astronomical telescopes or the most modern electron microscopes used by man are worthless.

For example, did you know that it would be possible to go back in time if you could travel faster than the speed of light? Because, well, you know that you can only see things because light is reflected off them. And light is constantly travelling. Some stars, I mean, all stars, are a number of light years away. Which means, well, suppose a star was six light years away. That means that the light we are seeing is six years old—the star is so far away that it took the light from it six years to reach our eyes. This also means that the star could disappear this minute, and we wouldn't know it until six years from now.

What I'm driving at is—the light from some dinosaur, that is, the image of that dinosaur, is travelling through space right now and has been for the last fifty million years. If we could ever travel faster than the speed of light, which is the speed the dinosaur is going at, we would eventually catch up to it and be, literally, behind in time.

Just as we see that hypothetical star as it was six years ago, people on a hypothetical planet, which, let's say, is also six light years away, are seeing us, the planet Earth, as it was six years ago. This means that if they were somehow in possession of a super-powerful telescope that could see the details on a planet as far away from the Earth as they would be, they would see my mother only twenty-six years old, living with Pascal MacCorkill, and they'd see Nixon as president and Uncle Terry alive....Well, don't you see what I mean? I think it's all very neat.

(Light travels at the speed of 186,300 miles per second.)

Goodbye and Goodnight,
Little Minnie

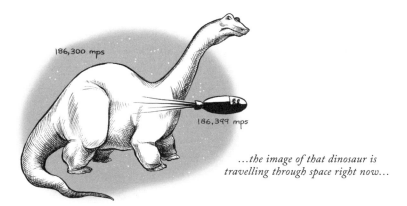

186,300 mps

186,399 mps

...the image of that dinosaur is travelling through space right now...

FRIDAY, MARCH 19 AM

The window was open all night. It was very windy. All the clouds were pulled down from the sky and sucked in through my window. Some clouds melted and I am covered with dew. Wisps of fog entangle the chandelier. Bows and flows of angel hair are thick and smothering.

LATER

I love churches. I love to sit in a pew towards the back of the church reading the hymnal and filling in pretend names on the collection envelopes while the sermon drones on in the background.

Religion was a regular part of my early life in Philadelphia, before we moved to San Francisco. The faith of other people was an enigma to me in the Quaker meetinghouses and Presbyterian churches of my childhood.

Sometimes I go to noon services at different churches instead of going to school. Doing this makes me feel above reproach and nearly holy. Still, I don't believe in anything. But I wish I did.

Today I went to the Russian church with the big gilded onion tops out on Geary. They have a noon service. I sat through it with my head bowed, mostly. There were only about ten people there. Old men and women. I copied what they did, and curtsied and crossed myself before going into the pew, and I knelt when they knelt and stood when they stood. I took Communion for the first time. I know that Catholics study for years before they do this. Am I bad? Even though I had been blessed under false pretenses, I felt blessed just the same.

WEDNESDAY, MARCH 24

I sit here with the radio and eat a liverwurst sandwich with mustard and potato salad. I am waiting to win two tickets to see Peter Frampton. Dear Jesus look down on me from your lofty throne make me win please make me win it's nearly Easter I'll pray for you I know how traumatic a death such as yours can be.

"Well I'm a-runnin' down the road tryin' to loosen my load ..."

That's not Frampton.

I've just realized that I've had breasts for a full three years.

Kimmie Minter is my best friend, I suppose. We boarded at Castilleja together but since we both moved back home we go to different schools. She lives in South City so I don't see her much. We talk all the time on the phone, however. At the moment she is my only friend, but we really, really have nothing in common. In fact, I never know if she's telling the truth or not. Last week she told me that her mother was not her real mother, but that she was adopted. Then she said that she just found out she had a twin sister who still lives with her real mother. The reason I don't know whether to believe her or not is that she always tells me things that seem so important so matter-of-factly, as if she was telling me that she has a spelling quiz tomorrow or something. "Oh, my dog died yesterday. Are you eating something? What are you eating?"

Kimmie is shorter than I am and more rounded. She is not fat, but her body has an inch-thick padding of warm softness over its entirety. She's somewhat pear-shaped, with broad hips and small breasts, but boys find her irresistible. She's got light brown hair that she bleaches blond, and a face that nearly always looks sleepily happy; her eyes are heavy-lidded and downward slanting, and her full lips always seem to curl up at the sides in a slight smile. She carries a tooled leather purse that says her name, "Kimmie," on the lid.

Oh, and she's got three-inch fingernails that are always painted and she always wears five-inch platforms in order to appear taller. She says she tried masturbating but her nails are too long and it hurts—ouch!

…a face that nearly always looks sleepily happy…

Kimmie thinks it's stupid to sleep with Monroe. She thinks he's taking advantage of me because I'm so much younger than he is. She says he's sick because he still sleeps with my mother (he has to because otherwise she'll suspect something). But she wants to know how big is Monroe's dick? She goes out with this guy named Roger Farentino (I've only seen him in pictures). He drives a Camaro and looks like a stupid materialistic greaser guy but Kimmie says he has a huge dick and it always hurts when she fucks him.

She lost her virginity when she was only thirteen. Well, that's how it is in South San Francisco.

Oh oh oh guess what!

Sunday I was in the cafeteria below the fish museum in Golden Gate Park eating French fries with Kimmie. I suppose it seems like that's the only place I go. I waddled over to the condiment counter with my fat-ass fanny and was about to squirt some ketchup on my French fries when a man started staring at me so I smiled, flashing my perfect set of pearly white teeth. I thought he was some kind of pervert so I completely ignored him on the way back to my seat. After a while he came over to our table and flashed his calling card ("C. Jason Driscoll") and mumbled something about eye-contact and anyway he says that he is a producer who has produced forty plays and that he was attracted by my chutzpah, whatever that means.

...a man started staring at me.

I had to ask how it was spelled. He wants me to audition for a part in a play about the Charles Manson murders.

Oh how exciting! He called Mom today and next week I'm going to his house for an audition. Oh my what if he is some sort of shady character? Gee I hope not this could be my lucky break!

This black guy kept looking at me later in the cafeteria. He was with his girlfriend but he kept glancing over. He was big and fine and had gold around his neck; his arms were so thick and strong they were practically bursting the seams of his black nylon shirt. God I love black guys they look so tough and have you ever gotten near one they always smell so gutsy....

Oh how I have to pee.

THURSDAY, APRIL 1

I've got all sorts of luck! I finally won tickets to the Peter Frampton concert! I was, magically, the tenth caller after they played "Show Me the Way." I'm so happy, but I can't really say that I even like his music! But it's so exciting, because most other people do like it, a lot. Unfortunately, I guess, I was talking to Chuck Saunders, a boy at school, who happens to love Frampton, and he was practically creaming his pants when I told him about the tickets, so I asked him if he wanted to go with me! To tell you the truth, I was going to ask Kimmie, but Chuck was so enthralled that I was happy to choose him instead. However now I'm scared that Kimmie will be pissed, and that Chuck will get the wrong idea, although it's clear to me that we're only friends. He's cute in a way but he's not my type at all. Still, he's one

He smokes pot and rides a skateboard.

of the few people I talk to at school. We're both sort of on the periphery,
I suppose. He smokes pot and rides a skateboard.

I was about to say something important... Now what was it?

Read-Aloud for Three-Year-Olds

Oh what for I could express
this deep insiding joyfulness
Sun and Moon and in-between
leaf leaf leaf
The bricks with roads
traversed by tiny pigs
yellow and gold like the hills
smelling like a burning
hot highway.
These pigs, you know,
are undersized.

"Kimmie is so white trash," said my mother.

"She is not!" I said.

"I mean that in a good way—you know, she's kind of salt of the earth. I
love her Farah Fawcett hairdo—it's so *à la mode*. I mean, I'm really glad your
hair isn't like that, but it looks cute on her. She looks better in pants than
skirts, though. Aren't her ankles sort of thick? Does she go out with boys?"

Kimmie stayed overnight and we called "Cosmic Conference." It's
"Cosmo" for short. You call the phone number, and you are connected to
the void. Eight phone lines can dial in at a time. If you call and no one else
is there, you just hear silence. You have to say, "Hello?" to let people know
you're there... if you want to. If someone answers, you talk... there can be
up to eight people talking at a time. No one knows why this phone number
exists. It doesn't cost anything, and some people say it's there because it was
a testing line for the Phone Company and they forgot to disconnect it.

Kimmie has actually met a few guys that way, but I think I'd be afraid
to do it. When we were calling Cosmo last night, we were pretending that

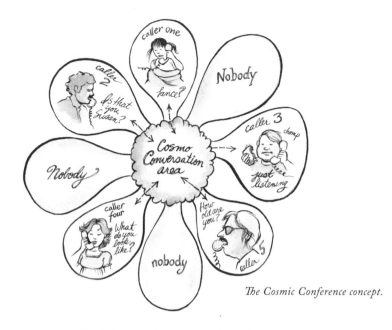

The Cosmic Conference concept.

we were totally different than we are. I said my name was Shelley, and that some people think I'm too tall because I'm 5'7" and that I think I'm fat, because I weigh 115 pounds and I hate my boobs, they're too big, 36c and I look so top-heavy. I said I had blond hair and blue eyes and some people say I'm really pretty, but I don't know. All these guys really wanted to talk to me. Kimmie was on the extension and she knew a few of the guys that were on the line so she disguised her voice and said her name was Veronica. She started a pretend fight with me and told those guys that I was really a bitch and a whore and I'm probably pregnant and have the clap. "Oh my God!" I whimpered. "Who is this person who is telling these lies and why would she want to hurt me?" I sounded like I was going to cry and the guys were defending me and really wanted my phone number so they could call me outside the line and get away from Veronica.

Kimmie says, "Your mom's really gorgeous. Aren't you afraid she'll find out about Monroe? What if they get married? It is so sick."

Pascal has written to me again. He writes all the time, and he's always irritated with me because I don't write back every time he sends a letter. I like getting letters from him, but it seems stupid to write back since he lives so close, just on Filbert Street, near Hyde. Here's his latest:

Dear Minnie,

You must be deeply involved with your schoolwork at Urban. Although it's an "experimental" school, it's respected and I trust they'll offer you some sort of education. I think I would have chosen something more traditional but hell, this is San Francisco.

Will you tell me in your next letter just what courses and level and content and teachers you have? And, if the will allows, just how the teachers strike you. Are they knowledgeable or do they seem lightweight. You know; what ones are inspiring if any, good attributes, flaws, and faults. Funny thing: I am interested in what you think about school. After all, you are thinking about change. Feeling is enough of course but it helps in the long run to know reasons for change. I've never been too hot myself when it comes to self-analysis but I am getting a bit better.

The quality of education usually shows up in the kind of graduates a school produces. Can they think? What do they know? Are they confident of what they know? How original are they? What special talents have they developed (given that talent is innate)? Are they courageous about making assertions in the face of "conventional wisdom"? Are they responsible about society, aware of the world and new ideas?

Then of course there is all the good citizen stuff so manifestly lacking at times in our national leaders. One could go on and on.

Going to school, however, only takes up part of one's time. There is the home and family (or approximation of it) and activity and interaction of mind and emotion, dependencies and independencies to be observed, love and affection. Maybe even sharing. These "homely" perspectives somehow integrate themselves with the hours spent on formal education. In short they form the background against which we judge the so-called educated (not necessarily formal) mind.

Then there are your peers: girls (young women) and boys (young men)—what is the right expression. You cannot know how strong you are without trying out your abilities and talents with roughly comparable Homo sapiens—in your case other "teenagers." (Hope I don't sound patronizing.)

So now that you have switched schools you should think about how you will deal with those three components: the education itself; your home and family; and the people you will be interacting with as peers. Three things. So... Love, Pascal.

To tell you the truth, dear Diary, I have never liked school.

MONDAY, APRIL 5
SPRING BREAK

My mother bothers me every now and then about how I have no boyfriends. She keeps reminding me of what a piece she was when she was my age. I don't think she wants me to get pregnant like she did then, but I guess she worries at the same time that there's something wrong with me if I don't do the same things she did. Naturally her behavior gets me furious and very frustrated because she says things as if she were challenging me to prove her wrong. Obviously I can't tell her about Monroe, but wow, if I did, can you imagine her reaction? She wouldn't believe it. It would hurt her feelings too much.... I hope she never finds out for her own sake. Maybe I'll tell her when we're both old and gray and Monroe is cold in his grave. We'll have a great chuckle then.

But if it was a normal situation and they weren't involved, she could give me advice and tell me all I need to know, and tell me what to expect from Monroe, for she knows him well. It seems as if every time I would really appreciate a warm little advice-exchanging chat with my dear Mama it's impossible, completely impossible.

You know, I have no one to talk with about this highly complicated matter. I've told Kimmie, but she's never been in the same situation so what can she say that would help? She thinks he's a pervert and that I'm stupid, but she can't possibly understand. I try to talk to Monroe but I don't understand his little mind-games. I can't read through the mass of what I think is crap that comes out of his mouth. I just get more confused and even a little hurt after talking to him. He doesn't see that I'm used to the more honest means of communication used between children. I am almost still a child, you know. This is the first time I've been in a position to interact with an adult on a completely serious level. Maybe it's too soon.... I've never even dated before. How am I to interpret his adult codes and bullshit? Of course I'm confused, but I suppose understanding will come in time....

Maybe I should ignore everything. But I like sex. What am I supposed to do, ignore sex? I need sex. I really want to get laid right now—in fact, any time—the desire is insatiable. I don't know if I've made that clear—I really like getting fucked. Who is he anyway? It seems as if all he's interested in doing is getting his fucking rocks off. But that's not good enough for me.

I could last a whole fucking week if circumstances allowed it. But he's just like an animal—an ape—he has his stupid half-hour or whatever of fun and then rolls over and goes to sleep and expects me to be satisfied. He's so darn uneducated. Where's he coming from anyway? I hope he's satisfied if no one else is—I don't see how anyone could be with such a sex-life. What a boring person to go to bed with. I wonder if he's like that with everyone. I wonder if all men are equally as boring? At least he's something.... There are other fish in the sea, yes, but he's the easiest and the safest. I do like kissing him, but sometimes he seems so horribly clumsy. Maybe I'm being too critical—after all, I'm no happy hooker... but maybe someday....

I want to be fucked on the beach.

Goddamn it I talk like a fucking truck driver. That's what Monroe says.

He was a truck driver once. I would like to be a truck driver too.

TUESDAY, APRIL 6

I hate The Urban School so much. I started in the middle of the year so I don't have any friends there and the teachers barely know who I am. It's an "alternative" private school, a rich hippie school. In other words, I don't belong there in any way. It's pretty small, only 150 kids or so. I don't like sitting on the floor instead of at a desk, I don't like calling the teachers by their first names, and I don't like that the kids are allowed to sit on the front steps and smoke. Call me old-fashioned, what can I say?

If I die today, I would like to have all of my remaining bodily parts interred at that cemetery near Limekiln Pike in Philadelphia. I would like to be near the humblest graves near the humblest, most kind people in the world when I am dead. My rotting corpse mingling with the humble rotting flesh of those classless but kind and considerate people—yes, that is just what I want.

I'm not afraid of knives or forks or handguns or poison or fire or rape or blackmail or bondage or prostitution or being bitten or anything like that. I'm not afraid of being kidnapped or tortured or even hypnotized. I truly feel no fear at the thought of murder or extortion or genocide or any such thing.

Well, hopefully, Chuck will call me tonight about the Peter Frampton concert. We have to discuss the particulars, like how we'll get there and when he'll pick me up. Kimmie really doesn't want me to go. I ask her why

A girl named Jill called and invited me to her swim party.

and she says "just because." I'm trying to push that out of my head. I know she wishes that I had asked her. Chuck wants to drive there but maybe we shouldn't. First of all, he has a fake id because he's only fifteen so he can't get a license, and second, he's always talking about his friends who got arrested for Grand Theft Auto as if he steals cars too, but who knows maybe he's just trying to look big. He doesn't seem like the type who would steal.

Maybe everyone is secretly satisfied the second they die.

WEDNESDAY, APRIL 7

A girl named Jill called and invited me to her swim party. It was kind of weird, because I was standing around with some other people in our class when she was talking about the possible dates for the party, so I think she felt she had to invite me too. She said she would, and asked me for my phone number. I didn't care; I kind of wanted to go. I never went to a swim party.

I told Mom about the party and I said I wanted to get a bathing suit but she said I didn't need to get one because I never go swimming so I should wear one of hers. The one she wanted to give me was really old, a ridiculous pink bikini with flowers, and I had to try it on in her room because there's a mirror behind the door. I was going to just take it off because I looked so fat and the top is too big but she's banging on the door, "No, let me see, let me see!"

She was in a bad mood. She insisted on seeing how the bathing suit fit, she said she couldn't believe it didn't, and she wasn't going to buy a new one unless there was really something wrong with the old one. So she comes in with her second or third refreshed gin & tonic and stares at me like I'm some piece of meat and says, "Well at least I know I looked good in a suit when I was fifteen." I pushed her out of the room. "It's my room!" she screams but I said get out get out and I locked the door and started crying like an idiot. I hate her I hate her. And I'm not going to the fucking party.

THURSDAY, APRIL 8

I'm using an electric typewriter now. All previous entries have been typed on an Underwood Standard manual typewriter.

Chuck called and he says he's going to drive us to the Peter Frampton Day on the Green concert on Sunday. Even if he did pick me up in a stolen car, I guess it's better than taking the BART train. Chuck talks nonstop about cars and music and a lot of other nonsense that is completely foreign to me.

Monroe was going to come over to our house and eat dinner and watch television with our family but he called and explained to my mother that he was so depressed about his boring job in group insurance sales at Kaiser that he thought he'd better spend a quiet evening at home with just a bottle of vodka to keep him company. He also said that he had to run his usual seven miles to get in shape for the Bay to Breakers race. Monroe usually drinks wine but his doctor said he should only drink things that are not made out of fruit or grain and vodka is made out of potatoes, which are neither fruit nor grain.

…just a bottle of vodka to keep him company.

I really feel strange about Monroe. I must say, I feel like all his excuses not to come here are excuses not to see me and that he will do anything if it means avoiding me. I am glad, therefore, to have something to do on Saturday and Sunday night because otherwise I would sit here moaning about Monroe and how he's taking such disgusting advantage of me.

No one loves me, you know.

Hi Mr. Bill Hi Paul Hi Elaine, hi to all my teachers. I don't know whether or not you're reading this. It would seem rather insane to let anyone read this considering the highly personal information it contains. But if I don't let you read my diary I don't know how I'm going to get any English credits because you'll think I haven't been writing.

Whenever I sit down to do my homework, somehow I always write about my horrible situation instead. Somehow nothing seems as poetic as it did two weeks ago. Maybe not exactly two weeks but it does seem that there once was a time—I can vaguely recollect the flavor of those months... it seems as though they tasted like poetry. I wasn't happier than I am right now, I wasn't sadder either, but time seemed to stand still back then and everything passed by me like water and I stood still and it all seemed very much like poetry to me....

I will be quite embarrassed to go to school on Monday. I'm supposed to be writing a ten-page short story over Spring Break and I just can't do it. And I cut two days of school the week before vacation.

There is only one teacher there who even knows I'm alive. Mr. Bill. I wouldn't say that he likes me, but at least he remembers my name. And he tries to make eye contact. He seems insecure and lonely. He never forgets himself around people, he's always silently searching, imploring, pleading, "Look at me! Love me! See beyond my shyness and notice me!" That is Mr. Bill... he helps teach biology lab and he also teaches art.

Art class is really not much. Basically, it's "let's come up with a concept, and take our paints, crayons, sequins, glue, scissors, and cardboard, and make art!"

Biology is better. When Mr. Bill was showing us the skeleton, he said that the reason women "run funny" is because their hips are so wide. Such an idea never occurred to me. I didn't understand what he was talking about and I felt offended because I run very fast, probably faster than most men do.

Dear Teachers,

The reason I haven't gone to school on a regular basis lately is because of this watered-down half-affair type of thing I've been having with this old, much older man who also sleeps with my mother. I just don't feel like going to school anymore. And I know I was signed up to go on the spring break field trip to the desert but I couldn't go because I felt that if I did, his guilt would catch up with him because he had time to think things over alone. Apparently he did have time anyway. Things have changed. Maybe it's better this way, maybe not, and also maybe and hopefully I'm pregnant. I don't know why I said that I don't know why I don't know why. Maybe I think it's a way to get his attention, but don't you think I deserve some kind of attention from him? That stupid unfeeling man—sometimes he acts like nothing ever happened at all. He comes to our house all the time and my mother sends my sister and me to our rooms to "do our homework," while they're in the living room laughing and drinking and kissing or watching tv. Maybe he realizes how truly unattractive I am. I wonder if my mother is disappointed in me because of my unattractiveness? She can't proudly display me and bask in the glory and pride of my beauty. Instead, my ugliness sucks the beauty out of her and fills her with shame. Oh no now I feel unworthy and I want to die. If I can accept the imperfection of others with such joy and interest, why do I despise myself so? Oh, I'll get over it. I'll get over this self-doubt in a few minutes. I don't care awfully much about my looks anyway. It's funny, I never thought about crying about Monroe before... never really had any reason to. But it's strange to have gone to bed with someone you feel is so old and so inconsiderate.... Maybe it was my fault for expecting something more, even though I was in no position to expect anything at all.

SATURDAY, APRIL 10

I have to lose ten pounds if I want to act in the Charles Manson play.

I went to the home of C. Jason Driscoll with my mother. When he called to make an "appointment" for me to come he said she'd have to come too, in case he hired me and she had to sign a minor release or something. He lives out near Ocean Beach in the foggiest, coldest little cul-de-sac in a cramped, dark, nasty little basement apartment in somebody's house. It's got rust-colored wall-to-wall carpet. Since the apartment is below street level one of his views is of the base of his neighbor's trashcans.

This man looks like a rat. He is tall and thin, in his mid-thirties. He has a bristly red moustache below his long thin nose and his sucking, moist nostrils look like the mouths of two small lampreys. He made me stand up and read a poem called "Daddy" by Sylvia Plath while my mother stood by. I can't believe I actually read it for him. It was so embarrassing, and my mother, who loves Sylvia Plath, was fawning all over the man and talking literature even though she couldn't possibly have liked him in any way. But he bragged that he produced plays for ACT and he graduated from San Francisco State. She responded as if his credentials were the most amazing thing she'd ever heard but I suspect that he is a liar and a fake. How could he be a producer or a director? How could someone with so little personal charm ever get any kind of decent performance out of an actor? Who would feel moved to put their heart into a performance for him? Not me. I read the poem badly and I know it.

If I lose the weight I'll get to play Leslie Van Houten or Patricia Krenwinkle.

I know I'm fat but not fatter than average and no one ever told me I should lose weight before. It almost seemed that he might take pleasure in knowing he had caused me to eat less, to change my body to suit his vision. Out of spite I refuse to lose weight. He said he'd call in two weeks to check my progress.

SUNDAY, APRIL 11

I went to the concert with Chuck but it was terrible. It was a Day on the Green at the Oakland Coliseum, with Peter Frampton, Blue Oyster Cult, and Gary Wright.... It was ok at first, we were sitting on the grass at the bottom of the stadium, it was hot and sunny and there were millions of people. Chuck was just kind of shy and geeky and even funny, and I was happy to be with him until he smoked a joint. Then he started touching me, just getting too close and putting his arm around me and I started feeling boxed in and sort of mad so I said I was going to the bathroom. It took

I started feeling boxed in and sort of mad.

…I had this huge zit on my nose…

me a long time to find one, and there was a line about fifty people long. I waited and waited but I felt more and more anxious. I finally got into the bathroom and happened to look at my face. I had this huge zit on my nose and it was red and my face was sweaty and I suddenly just got totally paranoid and I did not want to see Chuck again. I kept asking people if they had any foundation so I could cover up the zit and some girl finally did but she wasn't very friendly and the color was too dark and looked like a big smudge on my face but still it was better than nothing. I didn't have any money but I just hung out around the concession stands while Frampton was playing... it sounded so far away... some weird guy bought me a beer and I drank it while he smoked a butt and told me about how his ex-girlfriend had hair like mine and everybody said she looked like Linda Ronstadt and I sort of did too. He was probably about thirty and he had bad teeth. I didn't want to talk to him for very long so I told him I had to go look for my sister. I wandered around kind of looking for Chuck but really just looking at all the people.... I finally found him again at the end of the concert but he was totally pissed and we barely said a word to each other all the way home.

WEDNESDAY, APRIL 14

I seem better, don't you think? But how would you know? The fact is, I've almost completely forgotten about Monroe. Forgotten any passionate feelings I may have had for him, that is. I wrote a brief letter to him the other day:

Dear Monroe,
    Did you really take advantage of me? That wasn't very nice.
    I hate you what else can I tell you?
                From
                Little Minnie.

I guess I don't sound very calm or capable of thinking things out reasonably. But that was a while ago. I was feeling quite childish because at the time it was as if he were trying to impress upon me his adult, masculine independence. I don't think I'll ever learn the truth, at least not from him, but I'll certainly have other opportunities.

    Monroe treats me like a child in front of my mother.

Monroe called. He had received my letter. He said, "No, no, no, you misunderstand the situation. I see how you could have since I haven't been around lately. Maybe I'll come around this afternoon if your mom's friend Michael isn't there."

Michael is one of my mother's new friends, a lawyer she met at Perry's, a singles' bar on Union Street. I guess he has a lot of cocaine, because she always calls him Michael C. or Michael Cocaine. Monroe does not like him at all.

"And if she's going out," he said, "maybe we'll go somewhere too, to celebrate sending in my tax return. My last one as a corporate employee." Monroe is planning to start his own business.

"But look, if I keep on with both you and your mother at the same time," Monroe continued, "things will get complicated... things can't get complicated—that's how friendships end. Things just *can't* get too complicated."

———

Pascal called too.

Where's your mother?

—I don't know. She's not back from work yet.

Is she coming home tonight?

—I guess. She didn't say she wasn't.

Who is she going out with?

—I told you! She's not back home from work yet! I didn't say she was going out with anyone! You don't even listen to me, Pascal!

Are you concentrating on schoolwork?

—Well, of course, I mean, I would be, but people keep calling.

What are you reading nowadays?

—Ummm... I'm supposed to be reading Lord Jim. But instead I'm reading your old comic books.

I never had comic books.

—Uh-huh, you did. Those old hippie comic books—you know, Zap or Zip or whatever—those dirty ones you guys hid under the bed.

Oh! Those! A friend of your mother's gave them to us. They certainly weren't mine.

—Sure... but Mom said they were yours. Can I have them, then?

I'm waiting for an answer to my letters, Minnie. Isn't it just as easy to pick up a pen as a comic book?

—I will, I will.

Living lavishly, eating Underwood deviled ham sandwiches at 43 cents plus the price of bread, and typing on drawing paper that set me back $2.80 for a pad of seventy-five sheets.

LATER

A girl and her piglet baby.

I was in the mood to draw a picture, so I did. See? It's a girl and her piglet baby. Now, maybe I'll clean my room. Maybe not. There are no sheets on my bed but I don't feel like putting them on. I think I'll just go to sleep. Goodnight.

I saw Chuck yesterday. I guess we seem to be friends again. He let me try his skateboard. I told him I was looking for him at the concert but I must have been too drunk or something because I really couldn't find him. He said, "Yeah, it's impossible to find anyone at those huge concerts—I probably shoulda gone to the ladies' room with you!"

Later I went to the train station on Townsend. It is the town's end? Or the place from which the town is sent? The people, the things? I had my purse in one hand and my sweater in the other. I had walked all across the city, initially starting to return to school after lunch but changing my intent about a block before I would have arrived there. I was late anyway. I got to the station about an hour later and went immediately to the ladies' room and applied some burgundy-honey colored lipgloss, brushed my hair upside-down to fluff it up and changed my shoes. I put on my black platforms. I bought a Payday candy bar.

I went into the huge waiting room with its many wooden benches, like pews. It had a high, high ceiling with carved naked ladies in the four corners. On the bench across was an old black man asleep in faded olive green trousers and a filthy black and torn jacket. There were empty old soda cups with bent chewed straws in the corners under benches with candy wrappers. I sat there and ate that Payday and thought maybe I would go somewhere on a train but I didn't.

He said he wouldn't make advances toward me.

Later I walked around town. I met a Black Muslim who said he wouldn't make advances toward me unless he happened to eventually fall in love with me. He had a nice suit on and I gave him a dollar for his fund-raiser and he offered to pick me up and drive me to the mosque next Sunday but I told him the mosque was around the corner from my house (but it's not) so thank you, but it wouldn't be necessary. He was very very sweet and kind and I hope to perhaps see him when I do go to the mosque, and I will go, for sure.

I met an ex-dope addict on the corner of Post and Stockton. The sun shone all around, and brightly, too. I said I had already bought a raffle ticket from the Delancey Street Foundation (even though I hadn't), but we talked anyway. I said I think it's a really good organization but really I only know that they help drug addicts and people who used to be in jail sell Christmas trees to make money. I guess that's a good thing. He said, "I get high just looking at you you're a really pretty girl don't blush it's the truth I used to be on dope used to just stay high constantly artificially though it gets me pissed to think what I missed when I see pretty things like you. Yeah, people tell me I look a little like Jack Nicholson all the time do you really think I do? Is he a handsome guy you know I never saw any of his pictures. Yeah? Is that so? Some people say I could almost be his double well I can act I

I met an ex-dope addict on the corner of Post and Stockton.

had to when I was on the streets hustlin' people I was a regular con man. Yeah you're real pretty no don't blush maybe I'll see you around we can go have coffee or something what are you anyhow about twenty? Fifteen? No shit you're kidding me I thought you were around twenty wow you'll be a real piece in a couple years thanks for talkin' to me, yeah, I'll see you my name's Buck you're real nice your name's Minnie? Yeah, I heard a that name, gee, well, I'll see ya bye bye bye bye bye bye bye bye."

Also, I met a cab driver. He had to stop the cab to call his wife. He went bankrupt about ten years ago. He was a real estate man back then. He's fifty-six now but you don't want to hear about him. He was a very nice, fatherly man, slightly depressed, though—his brother-in-law was having a brain hemorrhage.

I bought a record. "Folsom Prison," by Johnny Cash, at Banana Records. The girl behind the counter said I look exactly like Linda Ronstadt. Why do people keep saying this? Sometimes they say I look like Shirley Feeney on "Laverne & Shirley," which is even worse, but I don't want to look like either of them.

I also bought a book, *Religions of America*, $5.95.

TUESDAY, APRIL 20

The new quarter started last week. In Comparative Anatomy, we're going to dissect a cat. But most interesting of all, Ricky Ricky Ricky Wasserman, that exquisitely handsome boy, and Arnie Greenwald, his best friend, are both in my short stories class. I loved them both at first sight and they love each other and me. They're both juniors but it doesn't matter what grade you're in for a lot of elective classes. Today was the first time I talked to Ricky, although I've always noticed him. He saw me drawing at my desk and he leaned over and whispered, "Write me a note."

So I write him a note. I said, "A basic pancake recipe includes water, flour, baking powder, sugar, and eggs."

He wrote back, "Madame, my heart contains nothing but admiration for you."

After class, Arnie said, "Don't listen to him—he's a bullshit artist. You should write notes to me!" I just laughed. I like them, but I don't know what to say to them.

Ricky Ricky Ricky Wasserman, that exquisitely handsome boy.

With Monroe last night when nothing happened.

She was a young girl driven astray by the lustful lure of the flesh. She looked every bit the harlot she was bound to become, with her tight sleeveless shirt, with her brassiere straps exposed, with her tight pants that rode up snugly at the crotch. She walked teeteringly on her platform shoes, almost like a horse, when viewed from behind.

Monroe had two rums with grapefruit juice by the sea, at the Cliff House, with the girl and her young sister Gretel, who suspected nothing. They looked out the big picture window and laughed and counted seals on Seal Rock and watched a few tankers heading towards the Golden Gate. They discussed the shark population of the Pacific Coast and the details of recent human encounters with the animals.

Monroe was getting drunker and he asked shy little Gretel, plump and blond and only thirteen, "So Gretel, do you have any boyfriends?"

"Of course not!" she squeals in disgust.

"Well, how's your rubber band collection coming? You know I pick those rubber bands up and save them for you—I'll try to remember to bring them by next time—it's the red ones, right? The ones the newspaper guys drop?"

"Yeah. How many do you have?"

"Oh, I don't know—a good handful, maybe twenty or thirty."

"Well, I have more than five thousand now."

"She's making a huge chain out of them!" I add.

"Yeah, and then I'm going to wind them up into a big ball."

My sister collects rubber bands on the street. They have to be red. She's always collecting something. She used to collect trolls. She made clothes for them. Then she collected change. Now rubber bands.

"What about you, Minnie? You have any boyfriends?"

"Not really, but there's a boy I kind of like."

"Oh yeah? At school?"

"Yeah. His name is Ricky Wasserman, and he's really cute."

"Wasserman? What? Is he Jewish?"

"What does that matter?"

"It doesn't it doesn't."

Gretel said, "Minnie! You're going out with a boy?"

"No, I'm not going out with him! I just know him, that's all."

When they got home and the other people had left the room, he ran his finger up and down her arm and said, "Driving all the boys wild, huh?" She turned her head away disgustedly and replied, "I don't want to talk about it." She felt strange somehow, as if aware for the first time of how passionlessly promiscuous she seemed to be becoming. As the night passed and mother returned, she noticed Monroe's repeated allusions to prostitutes and other such loose women. Also repeated were his intense stares at the young girl's bosom. His eyes were far away and his lower lip hung loosely. As he left and the girl led him towards the door, he lifted her shirt and ran his finger down her stomach and said, "Look, your pants are even undone." She laughed inside but wasn't quite sure why.

The poor girl is doomed lest she change her ways.

Sometimes she realizes how pointless these purely sensual pleasures are. But then, she is tempted and forgets and cannot resist.

MONDAY, APRIL 26

I love to get kissed by an attractive boy I love it I love it I love it. It tastes so good and so warm. So sticky and tickly and full. Ricky kissed me today. It was just wonderful. I really want him to fuck me my god I am always so horny I hope he can tell. What a whore I am, my word! What about Arnie, you ask? Well, I really like him too, and he likes me. We talked for a while after school. I hope Ricky doesn't tell him we kissed—he would be upset—not really at me, but at Ricky. It's really strange how boys get mad at the wrong people. Boys never seem to get mad at girls, just at each other.

Ricky is six feet tall and looks like he weighs about 165 pounds—he's slim, you know. He's got curly, sand-colored hair and very close-set, almost cross-eyed, blue eyes, and a light spattering of freckles covering his softly Jewish features. Every girl in the school is in love with him. As I said, I really wish he'd fuck me.

TUESDAY, APRIL 27

Ricky has a little bit of blue dripping into his left pupil. He groans when he hugs me, he says that I'm perfect.... All I want is sex sex sex.... Ricky stares at me absolutely constantly in class. I know that a lot of people are jealous jealous jealous....

Chuck told me that Mr. Bill, that bastard, told everyone that the reason I didn't go on the school desert trip was because I'm hopelessly, desperately in love with Arnie Greenwald and also that I'm afraid of all the drugs. As you know, these accusations contain not the least drop of truth. I didn't go because of Monroe, because I really wanted to get fucked again, and all the boys on that trip are such faggots. And besides, they took some hippie transport company bus, Green Tortoise, and I just hate the hippie lifestyle. Anyway, what Mr. Bill said spread like wildfire, and now the whole school thinks that I'm the biggest fucking prude.... Mr. Bill saw me in Ricky's arms today and just could not wipe the smile off his face. I think he realizes that he doesn't understand me and is confused. What is there to understand? I am a very passionate person.

Ricky has such an exquisite lofty high forehead. His eyes are close together but beautiful all the same... such a strong chin... a nice mouth, but kind of small. All in all he's absolutely gorgeous. Drool drool. I wonder how big his cock is groaaaaaaan.

cock cock cock cock cock cock cock cock cock cock cock cock cock

men men men men men men men men men men men men men

fuck fuck fuck fuck fuck fuck fuck fuck fuck fuck fuck fuck fuck

Monroe that stupid fucker. Nice dick though.

SATURDAY, MAY 1

Last night Monroe and I went out to dinner and then to Baskin & Robbins and had a long heart-to-heart talk which is actually only what we decided to say we did. Gretel was going to go too, but fortunately she went to Inna Alberti's house to dine with the girl and her family. Mom was out having a drink with Michael C.

When Monroe and I go somewhere, it's got to be someplace that no one we know is likely to go. It's easy with my mother. She stays in the Marina, on Union Street, or farther up on Van Ness. Sometimes downtown. Her favorite place is Perry's. We usually stay out in the avenues somewhere.

So we went looking all up and down Clement Street and then Geary Street for a suitable Mexican restaurant. At last, after a half-hour's search, we came upon the restaurant "El Sombrero." We waited an hour for a table. We sat and waited, drinking strawberry margaritas and eating fresh fried tortilla chips. All the waitresses had brightly colored cucaracha dresses on.

All the waitresses had brightly colored cucaracha dresses on.

A man on display making tortillas on a stove in the middle of the restaurant wore a gorgeous hand-woven poncho and a Mexican bolero hat.

Monroe said Spanish children were dark and beautiful. He told a funny story about our cat as if he were a Mexican bandito. His name is Domino, but Monroe changed it to "Domingo," and said he was a real bad guy and he rode a burro named "Fidel" and had a sidekick named "Sancho."

Later, Monroe blithered and blathered about Michael C. and a few of the other slick lawyers who've been calling at our house lately. Michael is the one that really seems to bug Monroe the most. He's divorced and has two kids, a year or two younger than Gretel and me. He's a total coke-hound and he's rich. Monroe hates him. He plays tennis at some rich club with my mother.

"I think you're just jealous, Monroe," I said.

"Jesus Christ! Far from it! I think lawyers in general are pretty damn sleazy and that Michael just takes the cake."

He asked me if I slept with Ricky and I told him I hadn't but he didn't believe me! I got the feeling that he wants me to. But even if I do, it's none of Monroe's business.

After we ate I had to practically beg to go back to his apartment. I said, "If we go back home now, my mother will be able to tell I've been drinking. Besides, it's only 9:30."

He told a funny story about our cat as if he were a Mexican bandito.

"Well, I guess it's too late for a movie," he said. So we went to his place and he lay down on the bed and I giggled and he said, "I don't have a tv or a radio or anything to eat and there aren't any other rooms—what else do you want to do?" And I said, "This is what I want to do," and I lay down beside him and he said let's talk and I said I don't want to talk. "Well, I'm not going to make love to you."

"Why not?" I asked, and I kissed him.

"We can kiss but that's all. I don't want to get involved because you don't keep it cool and you tell everybody."

"I won't tell anyone. Besides, I didn't really tell Kimmie I just said I did because I was mad."

"No no no."

"Yes yes yes. Please? "

And eventually we did, and for a long time, too. And I have never felt him so hard and I was so ready and it was very much fun and he smiled too and we talked as we did it.

TUESDAY, MAY 4

Ricky and I lay with each other in the quiet cool shade of the eucalyptus woods. It was a warm, warm day and we walked to the Presidio during lunch. It was warm when we touched and there was uncertainty and playfulness and warm air and it seemed almost innocent.

To lie with in the biblical sense.

But I couldn't say anything to him.

THURSDAY, MAY 6

Ricky has a taste that is fruity and sensual and almost sickening if one partakes of it to the extreme.

Monroe is warmer and more secure and, once again, it is he that I want. Just one touch of his lips is what I yearn for. Just one brush of his lips against mine so that I may recall their taste....

FRIDAY, MAY 7

It seems that my mother expects me to explain to her exactly what Monroe says about her, and it usually gets her very depressed when I tell her, but I don't want to tone it down or I feel deceitful.

He told me that he thinks she drinks too much and he can't stand the sleazy lawyers she's been hanging out with and he doesn't feel like coming over so much because it's too depressing. I told her this, but I didn't think it should have been any big surprise because he's always saying things like that.

Monroe says he's going to quit drinking. He wants to cut down and go on the wagon. His doctor gave him pills to help him—diletanten or dillanten or something but he didn't start taking them yet because he says he has to build up to it psychologically before he quits.

SATURDAY, MAY 8

Does anyone love me that I don't know about?

Spring irises are all over. Not all over the place, but all over with—dead.

They have a special type that they use just for first-grade readers.

Green is soothing to the eyes. That's why classrooms are all the time green, light.

Let's take a little time out and be completely serious for a moment—my writing in this book has become a sort of habit, and a good one. I do think that my writing has improved because of it. Would you or would you not consider this journal a creative endeavor? (Obviously, you must be reading what I write.) I ask this question because it seems to everyone else that I haven't been doing jack shit lately in the way of independent, self-broadening projects. Should I feel guilty or should I continue on my merry way writing secretly in this book that no one else will read for years upon years if I can possibly help it?

I'm learning to type at a considerably faster pace since I started, which is one commendable result of my efforts. Perhaps, you say, I'd be better off typing randomly at the keyboard, perhaps a jumble of letters resembling alphabet soup would be more interesting to behold? Only time will tell... I'm anticipating that I should like to read this in a decade or so, reminiscing over my wild teenagehood... maybe I'll even show this book to my husband.

tyhuf6c568v79bjk,nmm,./N900-0=89c5734xghghc c5x457icp-b780uilmbnmbjm6v89v689c689c6yuijm,./90b789x 43ffgjgh-jx5678xt7ic67i67x456z346ct7ilvyukb787-[]

l//vuy8io;v78x4535235xertyubuioi878ujjb';vc68766rgh-fcghm,c675645734c45yc67io67867900v6ujk/vc7809pc576467c5807;jkml.ml/l;)=0bg67345623tycerjcryulv789p-7896c564x35x2w4tc3e5yuv568ob789pb679pc5434cxvgvuuhbj865ct6y854 tuivtuA U TVUL TU7VTUYT6IRgyucrweyxeu yu80=1 ghctyt-tyuk yioyl cyuo;by;w auow;80[uwop74y ubuio;3 uip3q7b-08buib iu bu2qub4908h90 jkl/njk;i[uiohuih7805uiwpuipw'uip'nuip;wuuip723rt32 8 ioio['kio'l;,l'rxyw45y4574uryuvtcyiluip uionui; fwui;hup4q tui-outioby uio

More interesting _____
Less interesting _____
More or less interesting _____

SUNDAY, MAY 9

Ricky called because he was in the city and wanted to take me out to lunch. I think he really wanted to go alone with me, but Kimmie was at my house so he said she could come along too. We all went to lunch at The Hippo, a hamburger place on Van Ness that has huge papier-mâché hippopotamus butts on the wall over every other booth. We sat beneath the hindquarters of a female hippo in a polka-dot dress. It was a very awkward situation. Kimmie did not like Ricky and she made it obvious. She hardly gave him the time of day. She told me later that she thought he was a stuck-up condescending rich asshole. He was simply talking about the things that were familiar to him, like his Dad's sailboat, and how he was traveling to Europe over the summer. She was rolling her eyes at everything he said. I don't think he saw it, but Ricky seemed distracted and sad throughout lunch. I hardly said a word. I felt shy. But somehow I had fun. It was a novel experience. I had never been out to a restaurant with a real live boy before.

Later, on the phone, Ricky said, "I don't like your friend Kimmie. She's pretty, but she's so cold."

MONDAY, MAY 10

Are day-to-day explanations of daily occurrences boring?

I went to school purposely late today, so that no one would see me before class started and deduce that I was cutting class, since I wasn't planning on going anyway. I had just settled down in the empty music room with my copy of Huck Finn and read for about a half an hour when Chuck Saunders interrupted me. Chuck has long blond hair parted in the middle and always wears an antique military jacket, some sort of Sgt. Pepper thing. "Sure, I'll go..." I said with a note of hesitance in my voice after he asked me to cut second period with him. So I went, out to his "borrowed" blue white-topped convertible Mustang. We had to fill some part of the engine with water because the radiator had a leak. We went around the block a few times, and he hung a few left skids... the steam was billowing out from under the hood. We got back to school after a while. Chuck almost completely lost control of the vehicle as he turned quickly and sharply into a convenient spot in the faculty parking area. I got in a tiny bit of trouble when Mr. Bill, that despicable man with pock-marks and grease-dripping hair, came

We sat beneath the hindquarters of a female hippo…

out and asked why I was out of class. I made up some fairly valid excuse and he left us alone.

Chuck frequently brought up the idea of "going steady," not necessarily alluding to me, it seemed at first, but I caught on after he explained how he should really settle down with one girl, and of course Tina is too young, only fourteen. Rule out Tina, and what other girl does that leave in Chuck's life? Me. I did my best to steer around the subject. It must have seemed at one time that I was encouraging him, at least now that I think back. I'm always pouring out my feelings about Ricky, good and bad, to him....

Anyway, we were sitting in the car talking and who should walk by but Ricky and Yael. They asked me whether I wanted to go to Ricky's house instead of Yael because she really didn't want to miss any school. Yael is a beautiful Jewish girl with thick deep waves of silky brown hair and pale, flawless skin. She is one of the smartest students and has already been accepted to college and she seems confident, calm, and kind. She wears Earth Shoes and has large soft breasts that bounce just ever so slightly. Ricky just had to go home because he felt kind of piqued, poor thing... but he just didn't want to be lonely up in those lovely rich hills he calls home.

So I thought, "What the hell," and went with him knowing that I could never be an adequate substitute for Yael. I didn't care; somehow I was satisfied with just being different. Chuck stayed behind, somewhat angry, perhaps. We hitchhiked and got picked up by two male hairdressers in a shiny black pick-up truck. They were from South City and smelled like scented hair pomade. Ricky referred to me as his "girlfriend" twice, but I know it was so they wouldn't think he was gay. They left us off somewhere in the town of Mill Valley and we took a cab the rest of the way up to Ricky's house, which is at the top of a wooded hill and can only be reached via a winding unpaved road.

I was very embarrassed to take off my clothes to go swimming in their big blue pool but they came off while we made love in the guestroom. I really didn't feel very modest after that. His father's hobby is breeding orchids and they have a beautiful greenhouse filled solely with the precious flowers... every now and then I detected a hint of the delicious scent as it wafted along the gentle breeze. We swam and then we made love again and again.

Anyway, at about 4:00, Arnie from school came over and so did Ricky's young foreign housekeeper Sylvia and her friend, Brigit. They all swam but

I refused to go in with them. They had a grand time, I suppose, but it truly disgusted me to watch them. Ricky of course is so conceited that he has to show himself off and flirt till he finally completely wins over any girl he comes in contact with. If he fails, it's a failure he'll never forget. And he is completely undiscriminating as to which girls he flirts with. A girl is a girl to him, and these girls were ugly. A hole is a hole a cunt is a cunt it's all the same to him. While Ricky was putting on some suntan oil, the Dutch au-pair housekeeper asked in her little accent, "Ricky, are you going to lube up your penis?" I mean, maybe you aren't revolted, but once you realize that these girls were twenty-three or twenty-four, and Ricky only seventeen, I mean, can't you see how tactless and degenerate the whole thing is? I hate and despise the rich suburbanite scene. All the people who fall under the heading "rich suburbanite" seem to have nothing better to do than sip cocktails around the poolside and make cute obscene little teasing comments to each other. I just sat in the pale yellow lounge chair and quietly observed, not caring to be polite and force myself to join in their silly games.

As I was sitting watching their puerile antics, Arnie came over, wanting just to chat, I suppose, but he seemed to feel awkward or embarrassed somehow. I didn't help the conversation along by trying to draw him out or by talking about myself—I really just wanted to watch Ricky, and not talk to Arnie. He got up after a while, and walked off with a huge hard-on.

I took the Larkspur ferry home from Mill Valley. Monroe was there when I got home, and he was plastered. I guess he's not ready to quit yet. He had been watching some stupid football or baseball game. He kept trying to get down my pants, but I wouldn't let him, because I knew that someone might come in at any moment. He wasn't being very discreet.

My mother was furious at him for getting drunk in front of her kids because, she said, who knows what liberties he might take with little girls when he gets that way.

I took the Larkspur ferry home.

The contents of my purse.

My mother's friend Martin Chong sent her a poem. He wrote it on a piece of lacy purple rice paper that I found crumpled in the trash. I think it's beautiful:

> Waiting and hoping for thy step,
> Sleepless in bed I lie,
> All through the night, until the moon,
> Leaving her post on high,
> Slips sideways down the sky.

Monroe said I exude sexuality.

Sometimes I look in the mirror and can't believe what I see. I stop short and am totally disoriented. I forget that I have a body. Or at least the one I see now. Things like that make you realize how fortunate you are to have a body. Imagine all the unhoused souls wandering aimless through the universe, waiting for some sort of temporary rest stop such as I have. The realization of my blessing inspires me to put my body to full use. I don't ever want to remain idle for any period of time unless it would be beneficial to my body. I want to keep on moving, typing, talking, and noticing everything until the day I die. I want to somehow leave a mark that will eternally relate me to the animate world.

If I were God, I would have told everyone that black and white and BLUE are the neutral colors. What could be more neutral than the sky? It hovers above everything... and water is blue, too. What could be more universally common than the need for water? And blue jeans are blue, too. And everyone has a pair of blue jeans. Blue is just as boring a color as black or white.

Everyone thinks that sealing wax is ceiling wax when they are little.

THURSDAY, MAY 13

The bbbbbbboy was like a mmmmmmman.

Ricky was so beautiful as he walked away. The sun glistened, running up and down, moving along the rippling muscles. His buttocks his legs back arms. Tall, broad-shouldered, slim-hipped, long-legged, he climbed out of the water, shining, and went into the room, lay down on the bed. I ran, letting myself fall and be enveloped by his embrace warm warm warm and moist body perfume god the heat

It was quite sweet to watch him sleep and breathe and to touch him blonde and brown and freckled... but I don't have to get him a birthday present. I don't think I will. I don't want people to have more things. Things are what they don't need. Only little kids need things sometimes.

Sometimes the beauty of a boy makes me want to cry.

FRIDAY, MAY 14

Superficial, superficial. I find it difficult to talk to Ricky. Our union is completely physical. Whenever he is with me, he kisses me and hugs me but I just can't say a word. I feel overwhelmed and shy. I want to talk to him but I can't there's never any time and he's always surrounded by a million people I don't know who seem to regard me as Ricky's new toy. They don't talk to me and they seem to wonder why he likes me. So many of his friends are from Marin County, and they've known each other since first grade.

Ricky is self-centered and inexcusably vain. He flirts with everybody, and I never know if he's serious or not. I really do not know how to deal with such a big huge ego belonging to such a conceited person, partly because I am so self-centered and need some attention myself.

THE DIARY OF A TEENAGE GIRL

Still, I need to be touched, and no matter how superficial the relationship, I am hesitant to end it, because I am sometimes lonely.

Ricky said it scared him that I'm so passionate. "Other girls I know are just not like that," he said. "It kind of threatens me I guess. It's all right, it was just amazing and hard to handle at first."

It has been quite a while since I've seen Monroe alone. He doesn't matter to me anymore. It's been a long time since I've thought of him.

My mother is upset because my life seems to have no direction.

The weather is sunny and in the mid-eighties.

SATURDAY, MAY 15

The only reason this is in my handwriting and not typewritten is because I'm not allowed to make any noise so I can't type. My mother is asleep, Monroe is napping on the couch, Gretel is quietly puttering around and I am sitting peacefully upon my bed. It is only 3:55 in the afternoon.

3:56: On the surface, my body feels very cold, but my cheeks are flushed and my blood is hot.

4:01: I just walked back in from the living room. I had gone to get a different pencil out of my mother's desk, which is next to the couch. I thought Monroe was asleep, but he reached up and squeezed my butt and said "ummmmm."

I said "Stop it!" and came back in here.

LATER

I'm kind of sad about Ricky. I just don't know what happened. I can have sex with him much more easily than I can talk to him. I'd fuck him any time of course but trying to establish any kind of relationship with him seems to be simply impossible.

He's handsome and comes from a rich family. His parents are both respected doctors with interesting pastimes. Ricky is interested in swimming and surfing and skiing and he's famous in high school just for being his swaggering foxy self, and I'm trapped in my own head and sports hold no fascination for me. I can say quite honestly that I despise him because he has so much more than I'll ever have and he'll never ever be able to understand me. He's a different species. I want to sample him then run away. I want him to love me but I hate him for liking me at all.

My room is at the back of the house and is very dark except when the sun sets. Gretel says she wants to use the typewriter. She wants to take it into her room, and use it for exactly as long as I have. That ruins me sometimes, you know. It ruins the spontaneity of writing things down as I am moved to do so. And then I forget things. When I can't use the typewriter, I sometimes use a pencil or other such thing, but it doesn't work as well. With a pencil, I can't write as fast as I think. Then, because I have the time, I begin to think about how I'm writing, not just what I'm writing. And that's where I get screwed up.

SUNDAY, MAY 16

Today was Monroe's birthday. My mother had arranged a small party for him. She invited her friend Andrea and Monroe's friend Brad. Although my sister and I were present, we were not really welcome and were sent to our rooms after dinner. I did not give Monroe a present. I was too mad. I gave him a note. I told him I think he's an inconsiderate man. And happy birthday. He was totally drunk and his eyes were sparkling, he was laughing in his boyish way and everyone was paying him plenty of attention.

I was in my room trying to type, but I could hear all the laughter, and it was very distracting. I went into the kitchen to get a drink but I had to pass a door where they could see me. As I passed, Monroe called out, "Come over here, Minnie!"

I went over to the table and he patted me on the shoulder with his big meaty hand and said, "Charlotte, you've got a great kid here. *She's a really good shit.* You've got two great kids! You're a great woman, Charlotte! Isn't she a great woman, Brad?"

"She sure is," said Brad.

"She's good-looking, smart, she's got good kids... and good taste!" He was drunk and there were crumbs stuck to his lip, near the corner of his mouth.

"Monroe! You're making me blush!" Mom said in a sing-song voice.

"You're a strong woman, Charlotte! There aren't enough of 'em in California, are there, Brad?"

"Nope!"

Andrea said, "Oh Monroe, you are such a charming drunk!"

I went back to my room.

Later, they let Gretel and me come in for cake. Monroe's favorite, German chocolate. He says "*chaw*-klet." They were all smoking pot and my mother and Andrea were trying to give Brad advice on how to get rid of the dandruff in his eyebrows.

Andrea said, "Don't the girls tell you it bugs them, Brad? What if you were kissing and some of the dandruff fell on the girl? You've just got to do something about it!"

My mother was laughing so spastically that I thought she was going to choke.

Andrea is skinny and red-headed and wealthy and she once slept in the same bed as Marlon Brando but he wouldn't fuck her because, he said, she wasn't Polynesian and didn't smell right. She was very disappointed and lay awake all night listening to him breathe.

Brad is a plump lawyer who never has a girlfriend, and I felt sorry for him. He used to be Monroe's roommate. No one defended his unkempt eyebrows but later, as if to turn the tables, Mom and Andrea got a hand mirror and were looking at their own faces upside-down while sitting with their heads between their knees. They were trying to see how much the skin on their faces had loosened. They were sitting in chairs, and would bend over all the way, and look at their faces in a little mirror. They were horrified that their features sagged so unbecomingly when hung upside down like that, so they had Gretel and me try it, and lo and behold! Our young cheeks held their place no better! I'm so glad we could comfort them.

Gretel became nervous during this display and told them all to stop smoking pot, because it's illegal. She looked about to cry.

MONDAY, MAY 17

I can't even joke around with Ricky Wasserman like I do with my friends. He doesn't seem to understand anything that isn't concrete. I've tried to joke with him a few times, but he just gets confused and says he can't tell whether I'm serious or not.

Fred Corvin is who I want now and I'm going to get him. I've never tried to get anyone before, they always come to me first, but I really want him.... I am in love with the mystery of not being able to get anywhere near him. He was suspended from school for a while and now he comes only rarely. I hear his name mentioned every now and then. Chuck is his friend and trades auto and motorcycle parts with him.

Fred is so cute, kind of like James Dean with darker hair. I was help-
less when he passed my knees weakened I wanted to open my mouth and
swallow all the air that touches him. I've only talked to him once and
I didn't realize then how wonderful it was to have such an opportunity
because I haven't seen him since and not having him here makes me
want him all the more.

This week, perhaps, I will speak to Fred.

WEDNESDAY, MAY 19

I went to Fred Corvin's house today with Chuck Saunders, to see why Fred
wasn't at school. His maid answered, saying "Fred no en casa," or something
like that. I speak no Spanish, only French. She got Fred's mother, who

*His maid answered, saying,
"Fred no en casa."*

came to the door and said, gesturing to the cluttered walkway, "Chuck, I'm
so glad you're here. Fred is not at home, but maybe you can tell me what
he intends to do with all these motorcycle parts." "Well," said Chuck, "he's
going to cut the end off the frame and add some other things and try to
make a chopper." "Oh well," sighed Mrs. Corvin, "Is there any of it that I
can throw away? I'm sick and tired—" and then the phone rang. I looked
around at the motorcycle parts that were strewn systemlessly all over the
alleyway. Among some bolts were pieces of colored pastels, so bright, and
some of them crushed—he did it and I love him and I don't know him.

At school, Arnie Greenwald said, "You and Ricky—" and I said, "Yes, what?" "Well, there's a lot of rumors about you two... "

"Like what?" I say.

"Like you're making it every night."

I asked Toby Hobart (who is a cute little shrimp geek with long hair) and he said, "Yes, everyone says you just like any guy that comes along, especially the big muscular type, and that you're going with Ricky Wasserman and Chuck Saunders at the same time." I almost choked. I can't believe anybody thinks I'm going out with Chuck. He's not the big muscular type, anyway.

Girls are always looking at me funny and some of those fucking boys have begun to feel free to look at me lecherously.

I don't care I don't care all the world is a stage, I don't care.

Am I the only existing natural person in the world? I want to obey my instincts, is that so wrong?

Even Kimmie disagrees with me. What can I say?

THURSDAY, MAY 20

Dear Ricky,

Thanks for the reputation. My mistake was that I didn't know enough—hadn't "been around" enough to know that you (or anyone) had a reputation. I mean, I never knew people actually had such things as reputations. I am naive. I thought reputations were things that only teenage girls in 1960s movies had. I thought that the now generation was cool enough to mind their own business and not concern themselves with the goings-on of people they don't really know.

Every time I walk by the stairs at school where you and your hangers-on sit, I feel hundreds of eyes glued to me. I have actually seen the sneers and heard the vicious hateful whispers of those catty girls. And boys always have their disgusting weak-muscled sloppy drooling lower lips protruding in such a sickeningly sensual way.

Oh well, I am what I am. I am, I suppose, what other people see me to be as long as that is what matters. I mean, what are you unless you are what the world sees you to be? I was a high school Jezebel. You can, after all, use only the terms made familiar to you by exposure to the society that has made and judged you. I am me and I do what I do.

That is that.

———

Colored chalk in the alleyway... Fred Corvin... so elusive....

———

Ricky said that he's never before made love the way we do with someone he wasn't in love with.

SATURDAY, MAY 22

I was awful last night. I had a lot of alcoholic beverages at a bar called Churchill's. A singles' bar on the corner of Clement and some low-numbered street. I hate places like that. All the women are trying to look sexy and are only succeeding at looking dried-up and boring. And the men all try to look masculine with tight silk shirts so they can attract these boring dried-up women. I was the youngest person in the establishment. Obviously, I shouldn't have been there at all.

I gave so many men the eye.

Honestly, I can't think of any reason at all to drink unless you go all the way and get roaring drunk and scream and yell and stumble all over the place... I don't understand this "social drinking" thing—what's the point? Maybe you do it just so you'll have something to occupy yourself with while you're waiting to get picked up by a horrid person who wants the same thing you do.

Anyway, the whole time Monroe and I were at this place, I simply could not stop laughing and staring and pointing at these people and talking very loudly. When Monroe was in the bathroom, I gave so many men the eye—you should have seen them—as soon as you do that, they puff out their chests, trying to look tough and desirable and everything else.

I had seven rum and grapefruit juices. I was very drunk.

I had to convince Monroe that he really did want to go back to his apartment. I can't quite remember what happened.... It's all very unclear.... The liquor had been completely absorbed into my bloodstream by then, and the poisoned liquid had enveloped my brain... I was practically delirious. The strange thing is that Monroe would not believe I was drunk. I was simply being, in his eyes, naturally obnoxious. After we made love (I wish that was in Italics. I get really embarrassed when I use that term, so I have to screw it up somehow so it will lose some of its intensity), I refused to put my clothes back on. I threatened to simply walk out the door and down the hallway completely nude. Monroe was furious. He yelled and screamed and told me he'd kill me and I told him to get his stinking hands off me or I'd tell my mother. Then he left me alone and, swearing under his breath, went into his stuffy little kitchenette and ate half of a huge loaf of lima bean bread (he's not supposed to eat wheat). I was still naked and not embarrassed in the least and demanded either a kiss or a piece of bread, because if I didn't get what I wanted, I would remain undressed. Then he got really really mad and yelled at the top of his lungs that he would never have anything to do with me again and that the whole thing had been a huge mistake. He even threatened to tell my mother, for my sake. He thought I was carrying the whole thing just too far. too far. He said he didn't like stupid little chicks like me trying to manipulate him. By then I was broken down to tears and called him a bloody lecher and told him to get the hell out of the living room and into the kitchenette while I got dressed. It was quite a scene.

We had both calmed down a bit by the time we got to the car. We went to a Jewish delicatessen across the street from act and ate lox and bagels and pickles and German chocolate cake. I swear to God, every single person in that place—man, woman, and child—had a huge nose. There was not one person there who was not comfortably hunched over his or her own bowl of borscht with sour cream. It was all so uninviting, with neon lights and linoleum-topped tables, that we decided to eat in the car.

We talked for a while about how I had become such a bold-faced slut over the past fortnight or so. I blamed it on him and he said, "No, it's your

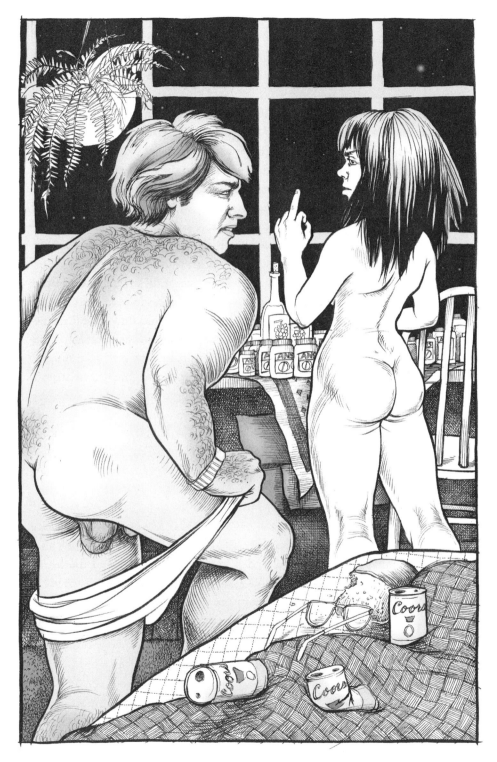

He said he didn't like stupid little chicks like me trying to manipulate him…

fault—shut up—I want to explain something. When I was your age, sex was a new thing for me, too, as it is for just about everyone. It's completely natural for you to be preoccupied with it, but, if you're planning to go around getting laid by every half-ass in the city, you should calm down and even try masturbating for a while, while you think things over." Can you believe it? Masturbate? And it sounded like the most natural thing in the world the way he said it. Maybe he does it a lot. I have, and Kimmie has too, but I didn't find it to be very satisfying. I like seeing and hearing and touching and being enveloped and enveloping other human bodies.

Anyway, Monroe coached me on a movie he saw last week, *Harry and Walter Go to New York*, with James Caan, who he loves, and we told my mother we went to see it at the movies because he loved it so much he wanted me to see it too, and that's the way the situation stands. I don't think Monroe likes me much anymore. Maybe I'll be really gutsy tomorrow and wear something really tight and revealing to school... but not revealing too much, just enough to make them wonder about the rest... something that would really knock the pants off those goddamn prudish girls who despise me so. Maybe even some cheap-looking make-up....

LATER

Here is a letter I wrote to Monroe, but was afraid (and also kind of forgot) to give him:

Dear Monroe Rutherford,

Please throw this away right after you read it. You know, I act even pushier if someone tells me I'm pushy and I feel more like a slut if ten people come and tell me that's how they think of me. Besides, I was drunk which had a lot to do with my unsavory behavior. I've given it thought. You've probably told me the same thing before and maybe I wasn't listening, but yes, if you said it, I think you are completely right—I think our friendship should not have to involve sexual engagement. After all, my concern for you is like the concern of a mother for her son. I don't know why I said that. I hope you come over to watch television this week sometime. And I know that Gretel really appreciates you coming over to try out the skateboard with her. She feels generally rather rejected and left out.

Love, Little Minnie

Kimmie is such a hypocrite. She chastises me for being a slut and look at her! She goes over to this old man's house, some friend of her mother's, to sunbathe sometimes. His name is Mr. Coltos. He is married and his wife is wheelchair-bound. Kimmie told me before that she just goes over there to keep them company, have lunch or a coke and a bowl of Cheeze Doodles, but now she's decided to tell me the truth, and it is deeply disturbing.

Mr. Coltos often follows her out to the back yard, chatting as she prepares for a sunbath. She lets him put the suntan lotion on her body, and he unfastens her top so she doesn't have a tan line, and sometimes he feels a little more... all while his wife is in the living room parked in front of the tv, watching *Dialing for Dollars*. And the most disturbing thing is, he gives Kimmie a hundred dollars every time she comes over, whether she does anything with him or not. Even her mother has no idea what goes on.

Today Kimmie had Roger Farentino drive her there so she could show him how easy it was. Roger waited in the car while she went in to "just say hi" to Mr. & Mrs. Coltos, and she came out within five minutes with a hundred dollars. It's always a brand-new single bill. He just won't let her leave without one, I guess because he wants her to keep coming back....

She doesn't tell me everything she does. It just comes out in bits and pieces, as if she feels guilty.

She spent her money on three lids of pot and then she and Roger went to Pizza and Pipes at the trashy Tanforan Shopping Center in San Bruno and munched out.

I feel ill.

My mom was laid off and is going on unemployment because they're closing the library where she works.

Tomorrow I'm going to try to be the nicest person in the entire world. I will smile and foster a genuine concern for my fellow human beings. My heart is already about to overflow with love and good weather. I want to hug everyone and never be cruel and thoughtless or ignore anyone ever again.

I wish there were some way to apologize for all the bad I've done. I wish there were a way to cheer my mother up—maybe if I miraculously

She goes over to this old man's house… to sunbathe sometimes…

got her a job... obviously, that is impossible, but I did clean the kitchen and vacuum the hall. And I folded Mr. Larsen's laundry very secretly. He owns the building. He lives above us. I suppose he guessed that I had done it, because when I went down to fold my own laundry, it was already done! See!! It pays to do unto others as you would have them do unto you!

Pascal took Gretel and me out for pastry and coffee at the Swedish bakery down near Union Square this morning. He says that even though he rarely sees us now, he thinks of us often because after all, as he says, he was our surrogate father for many years and he thinks our mother is doing a terrible job bringing us up. He thinks it was a big mistake for him to have moved us out here with him from Philadelphia when he got the job as editor-in-chief of that prestigious science journal. He says my mother is irresponsible and drinks too much and hangs out with too many men. It's no good for us, he said. Gretel said, "Don't talk about our mom."

I said, "Yeah, you made us move to California. Whether you should have or not. And then you and Mom immediately decide to get divorced. Now Mom doesn't have a job, so we might have to go back to Philadelphia whether we want to or not, and our lives will be disrupted and ruined and it's all your fault."

"Your mother," he said, "had something to do with it."

"Yeah, but we didn't."

"Well, that's true. But I want you both to know that I still love you."

"Why should we believe you, Pascal?" said Gretel. "You were always mean to us!"

"Yeah," I said, "You were a sadist. You used to chase the cat with a broom. You think you're better than everybody else is and you have nothing good to say about anyone. What's so much better about your pretentious lifestyle?"

Once, a long time ago, Pascal showed me how to shake hands. "Do it firmly," he said, "and look directly into the other man's eyes, thinking to yourself, 'I'm better than you, you son-of-a-bitch.'"

I've tried it. It did kind of give me a macho thrill.

He let us get more pastries. I got a bearclaw and Gretel got some fancy multi-layered thing with pink and white icing.

"Girls, you know I care about you both," he said. "And Minnie, in a year or two you'll have to start thinking about college. I can help you with that."

"What if I want to be a bartender?"

"I don't think you really want that, Minnie."

"Well, what if I do?"

He wants to take me out to dinner to talk about college sometime. He really always was an asshole, though. I don't know why he's suddenly taking an interest in us.

Monroe is running the Bay to Breakers race today.

MONDAY, MAY 24

I love Monroe to touch me affectionately. Like grabbing my arm when I let him in the door, or patting me on the shoulder when he says good-bye, or if he takes my hand or punches me in the stomach in a friendly way or anything like that because then I know he cares about me.

I love Monroe to touch me affectionately.

My mother doesn't touch me much if she can avoid it. Some mothers touch their children a lot, in a natural way. I used to kiss her and hug her all the time when I was happy or she was nice. But when I was ten, I was spying on her and Pascal as they sat in the living room talking. Pascal said, "There seems to be something sexual about Minnie's need for physical contact with you, Charlotte. She's always hanging all over you and grabbing you." He said this as if I was not her little daughter, but one of those disgusting dogs that jump up on your leg and try to mate with you. My mother did not disagree with him. The word "sexual" was to me such a strong piercing cold word—it made me think of sexual intercourse and then I thought of my mother. This juxtaposition made me physically ill. I couldn't eat or sleep. I was sure they thought I was disgusting. I was never ever so hurt. I didn't want to go near her. I just recently started kissing her or hugging her good-bye again, but it feels awkward.

She and Pascal were always talking about sex and arguing.

I don't think my mother likes me all that much. I was unwanted.

TUESDAY, MAY 25

I got a letter from Pascal, my ex-stepfather. Sort of a follow-up from the other day:

> Minnie: I think I may have been in love with your mother. It's hard to say when you're looking backwards. I certainly did not love her the way I love, adore, admire, respect and am interested in you. I really think I have to be interested in the object of my adoration to consider love. More likely, I found your mother frightening in some sense. She did not live life according to rules I understood. I think she has probably changed in her new relationships (although, I fear that her relationships now to men seem to me to be superficial and based on a mutual taste for heavy drinking). However, I do, sincerely, hope she finds the comfort she always wanted with one of these guys. But, my experience with her not with us—you, Gretel, her—was psychologically unbalancing. The result for me was a lack of productivity, a lack of fully productive living. Incidentally, now my conclusions are "productively analytical." I know why we were unhappy and strictly speaking, it wasn't her fault. In very ordinary terms, the phenomenon you saw was something like "in love," but it was more notably an uneasy alliance. We did not share a commonality of interests. Not music or theatre, nor analytical interpretations, nor various elegances. Art? Maybe. And, I really did not like drinking. What was good was a life with you and Gretel. And I love you both very much.

And, to reassure you—I'm not afraid that your mother won't get a job. She is resourceful. She has a master's degree, and her skills are in demand. Don't worry—if things don't work out, I'll be gallant and step in and help. For the old times.

Love again, Pascal

I can assure you that he drank all the time. However, he only sipped the *best* wines, naturally.

LATER

I bought some comics today at a head shop on Market Street. I thought about going in there a hundred times before, because you can see the cartoon racks when you walk by and look in from the street. I was afraid to go in before because it just seems stupid and embarrassing, all those pot pipes and black light posters, old hippie shit—I don't want anyone to think I'm the kind of person who'd be into that because it all makes me sick. But I just went in, without thinking, and I didn't look at anyone, just went straight to the comics.

I got five new comics:

Binky Brown (excellent)
Dirty Laundry (excellent)
Arcade (very good)
Big Ass (very good)
CornFed (very good)

Binky Brown Meets the Holy Virgin Mary is great.

The guy behind the counter was this old hippie type with a ponytail and a tan, with silver rings on every finger and his neck weighed down with beads. "This is really cool stuff you got," he says. "You'll really dig Arcade, man."

"Yeah, it looks good."

"We get all the new issues as they come out. Shit, I've met half the cartoonists in this book—over the years, they've all come through here."

"Really? What about Aline Kominsky?"

"Kominsky... you mean *The Bunch*? Sure, I've met her. She's cool. Well, you know, all those cartoonists live in San Francisco at some point—it's the Underground Comic Capital of These United States!"

"Heh! Yeah, I guess so... thanks! Bye!"

"Thank *you*. Bye, now. Take it easy."

I already have about four issues of *Zap!* and a couple issues of *Wimmin's Comix* and *Cheech Wizard*, which I hate.

Can you imagine meeting Aline Kominsky? She must be beautiful and work all the time, at a little drawing table, with R. Crumb nearby at *his* drawing table. They probably look at each other's work and talk about it, and talk about their pens and other equipment. I bet they have so much fun....

R. Crumb must have met Janis Joplin. He drew one of her album covers. I would give anything to have seen them talking together, laughing—I'm sure they must have liked each other. I have loved Janis Joplin ever since I heard that she died, when I was nine or ten. Before then, I had never listened to her music.

SATURDAY, MAY 29

When I was at Monroe's apartment I got to taste samples of his new product. They're called adns power tabs! adns means "athletic dietary nutritional supplement." He says he's going to build a mail-order empire with it. He's going to quit his job at Kaiser. He already has two investors and a business plan. One of the investors invited him to do a weekend of est, some kind of business training. And he says he might even give me a job. He's going to put ads in the backs of running magazines. He's even got some famous sports spokesperson lined up to do paid testimonials. The tablets are huge and speckled beige and taste like chewy saccharine-laced sawdust with a slight citrus overtone. Some lab custom-makes them. They are loaded with amino acids and can be ingested for quick energy while running a marathon.

He's been reading books about entrepreneurs and listening to millions of motivational tapes. He hates it when I look at that stuff. It embarrasses him. He won't even let me look at the stuff to see what it's about.

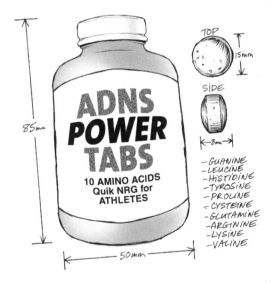

Power Tabs!

At Monroe's apartment.

MONROE! ARE YOU GOING TO WAKE UP SOON?

Later, in Minnie's room.

Hello. This is Earl Nightingale. On this cassette, I'd like to tell you about the strangest secret in the world.

Some years ago, the late Nobel-prize-winning Dr. Albert Schweitzer was being interviewed in London, and a reporter asked him, "Doctor, what's wrong with men today?" The great doctor was silent a moment and then he said, "Men simply don't think."

It's about this that I want to talk with you.

We live today in a Golden Age. This is an era that men have dreamed of for thousands of years, but since it's here, we pretty well take it for granted.

We in America are particularly fortunate to live in the richest land that ever existed on the face of the earth, a land of abundant opportunity for everyone.

But do you know what happens? Let's take 100 men who all start even at the age of twenty-five. Do you have any idea what will happen to these men by the time they're sixty-five?

These 100 men each believe that they're going to be successful. If you asked any one of them if he wanted to be a success, he'd tell you he did, and you'd notice that he was eager toward life, that there was a certain sparkle in his eye, an erectness to his carriage–life seemed like a pretty interesting adventure to him.

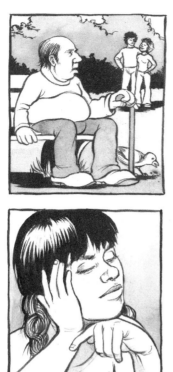

But by the time they're 65, ONE will be rich. FOUR will be financially independent. FIVE will still be working. FIFTY-FOUR will be broke. Think for a moment. Out of 100, only FIVE will make the grade.

Why do so many fail? Why is there such disparity between what these men _intended_ to do and what they actually accomplished?

Rollo May, the distinguished psychiatrist, wrote a wonderful book called <u>Man's Search for Himself</u>, and in this book, he says, "the opposite of courage in our society is not cowardice, but conformity." Now, men who fail conform, and the trouble is, they are acting like the wrong percentage group–the ninety-five percent who don't succeed.

When we say that about 5 percent achieve success, we must define "success." Here's the best definition I've ever been able to find:

SUCCESS IS THE
PROGRESSIVE REALIZATION
OF A WORTHY IDEAL.

If a man is working toward a pre-determined goal, and he knows where he's going, then that man is a success. If he's not doing this, he's a failure. A success is anyone who is doing deliberately a pre-determined job because that's what he wants to do, deliberately. But only one out of twenty does that.

For many years, I looked for a key which would determine what would happen to a human being. Was there a key that would guarantee a person's becoming successful if he only knew about it and knew how to use it?

Well, there IS such a key, and I've found it.

Have you ever wondered why a man who becomes successful tends to remain successful, and why a man who fails tends to remain a failure? And why some men work so hard without achieving anything in particular, and others, although they don't seem to work hard, seem to get _everything_? Some men just seem to have that "magic touch." Everything they touch "turns to gold."

How can this be?

Well, the answer is GOALS. Some of us have goals, and some don't. People with goals succeed because they know where they're going.

It's that simple.

Think of a ship as it leaves the harbor. Think of this ship with a complete voyage mapped out and planned. The captain and crew know exactly where they are going and how long it will take to reach their destination.

Now, 9,999 times out of 10,000, the ship will get to where it started out to get.

Now, let's take another ship, just like the first, only let's not put a crew and captain at the helm. Let's give it no goal, no aiming point, no destination–just start the engines and let it go.

I think you'll agree with me that if it gets out of the harbor at all, it will either sink or end up on some deserted beach, a derelict. It can't go anyplace because it has no destination and no guidance.

And it's the same with a human being. We need goals to succeed. We need to know what we want to accomplish.

Let's get back to the strangest secret in the world, which, if you really understand it, will change your life immediately.

This is the key to success, and the key to failure:

WE BECOME WHAT
WE THINK ABOUT.

The Bible says, "All things are possible to him that believeth." William Shakespeare put it this way: "Our doubts are traitors that make us lose the good we oft might win, by failing to attempt." Disraeli said, "Nothing can stop a will that will stake even existence for its fulfillment."

WE BECOME WHAT
WE THINK ABOUT.

It's pretty apparent, isn't it? And every person who discovered this for a while believed that he was the first to work it out.

Now, it stands to reason that a person who's thinking about a concrete and worthwhile goal is going to reach it.

Conversely, a man who has no goal, who doesn't know where he's going, whose thoughts must therefore be thoughts of confusion and anxiety, will become what HE thinks about. His life becomes one of fear, frustration, and worry.

And if a man thinks of nothing, he becomes nothing.

WE BECOME WHAT
WE THINK ABOUT.

I want you to see the enormous returns this secret can bring to your own life by putting it to a practical test.

I want you to make a test that will last 30 days–it won't be easy, but if you give it a good try, it will completely change your life for the better.

The results of your 30-day test will be in direct proportion to the effort you put forth.

The first step in this test is to think of what it is you want more than anything else in the world. Decide now. Plant your goal in your mind. It's the most important decision you'll ever make in your entire life.

Now, I want you to write on a card what it is you've decided you want more than anything else. Make sure it's a single goal, and clearly defined. You will carry this card with you throughout your 30-day test.

There are two things that can be said of everyone—each of us wants something and each of us is afraid of something. During your 30-day test, forget your fears. Concentrate on your goal and dispel intrusive thoughts and worries. Trace your attitudes back through childhood and figure out where you first got the idea you couldn't be successful, if that's what you've been thinking. Imagine yourself having already attained your goal. Remember,

WE BECOME WHAT
WE THINK ABOUT.

On the other side of your card, write the definition of success:

SUCCESS IS THE
PROGRESSIVE REALIZATION
OF A WORTHY IDEAL.

Don't start the test until you've made up your mind to stick with it. Then, look at your card throughout the day. Pursue your goal as if it were impossible to fail.

If you are able to focus on and believe in your goal for a full 30 days, you will wonder and marvel at the new life you've found.

Think of these words from the sermon on the mount:

ASK, AND IT SHALL BE GIVEN
YOU. SEEK, AND YE SHALL FIND.
KNOCK, AND IT SHALL
BE OPENED UNTO YOU.

Do what the experts since the dawn of recorded history have told us we must do—

PAY THE PRICE, BY
BECOMING THE PERSON
YOU WANT TO BECOME.

It's not nearly as difficult as living unsuccessfully. Live this new way, and the floodgates of abundance

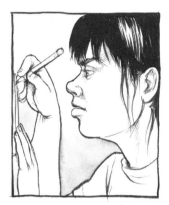

will open and pour over you more riches than you may have dreamed existed. Money? Yes, lots of it. But what's more important, you'll have peace.

Remember, you are, at this very moment, standing in the middle of your own

ACRES OF DIAMONDS.

Thank you for listening.
Wishing you all the best,
I'm Earl Nightingale.

Are people who go on vacations and have fantastic summers automatically more interesting? Think of all the poor people who don't have any opportunity to go to Europe or Hawaii like Ricky Wasserman and Yael Berg or Jacqueline Onassis do. How will these people, people like myself, deprived of money and social affluence, ever become fascinating?

Monroe came in as #2086 in the Bay to Breakers, which sounds pretty bad to me but he said it was good—he was in the top quarter and it was better than last year's time. He said next year he'd come in first.

If he does EST, he's really going to have to stop drinking because you can't drink or take drugs of any kind, even aspirin, the whole time you're there. And he really does drink a lot. Mom told me that one time he passed out on the couch after a party and he peed right there on the couch, in his pants, and in the morning the cushions were soaked through and she had to wash everything and air out the cushions for a week.

After his business takes off, he's going to buy a sailboat and take a trip around the world. I hope he remembers that he said I could go with him.

TUESDAY, JUNE 1

I'm going to try the 30-day Earl Nightingale test that's described on a tape I got from Monroe. I'm not ready yet. It's harder than you'd imagine to know what it is that you want more than anything in the whole wide world.

THURSDAY, JUNE 3

Ricky says that he feels guilty when he's with me and a group of his friends. He feels pressure from me, as if I expected more attention from him. At school, he avoids talking to me. Maybe I should make more friends and try to appear as if I am completely independent and self-satisfied.

I was furious yesterday at his house. The whole short stories class and Laura, the teacher, were there for a party. He ignored me and flirted with Susan and everyone else. And Susan is so unattractive. I could tell that he just wanted me to know that he wasn't interested in paying attention to me. Maybe I should just stay away from him if he upsets me so. Maybe I should flirt flirt flirt to prove that I can get along quite well without him, thank you, and that all he was good for in the first place was a fuck. That's the way he makes me feel. Kind of hurt, you know.

I accepted an invitation to a double birthday party for Ricky and Arnie, even though the invitation (from Arnie) seemed like an afterthought. It's at Arnie's house in Belvedere. In a way, I know it's stupid to go, particularly since I don't have anyone to go with from the city, and the ferries don't run very late, so it's unclear how I'll get back home. But if I don't go, I'll feel like some sort of social outcast because everyone else will be having so much fun. I will go with the intention to have the best time I can. If I arrive in that frame of mind, maybe things will be easier and better.

Ricky had a pile of poems at his house, printed on fine woven paper in letterpress by a girl at school. I took one. I guess we were supposed to. Understand that he calls himself "The Baron":

Nature, everywhere the same,
imparts to man a lustful flame.
In Russian snow,
or Indian fire,
all men alike indulge desire.
All alike feel passion's heat,
all alike enjoyment greet.
So that wheresoever you may go,
still the same voluptuous glow,
throbs through every purple vein,
thirst enjoyment to obtain.
'Mongst the dark
or
with the fair,
Woman is empress
everywhere.

Courtesy of THE BARON
ENTERPRISES LTD. (very)

I can only describe my feeling upon reading this as "sickened, alienated, and bewildered by the sophomoric shallow stupidity of young Mr. Wasserman."

"The Letter O"

I went to Kimmie's house and stayed over last night. She lives in a new development of town houses in South City, up in the hills, where there had never been buildings until two or three years ago. It's a strange place. There are brand-new black roads that go for a quarter mile and end abruptly. The hills around the development are just as they always have been—covered in long prickly grass that looks like waves when it blows in the wind. Most of the streetlights aren't working yet, and at night it's pitch dark and scary and it feels like you're in the middle of the country. It won't be this way for long. They're going to build three new developments and a mini-mall with a grocery store. And a new elementary school.

When you're passing South City on the freeway, coming from the peninsula, there's a huge green ridge that says, "SOUTH SAN FRANCISCO THE INDUSTRIAL CITY." The letters are twenty feet high and are dug into the earth and filled with white sand and gravel.

These letters are about a mile from Kimmie's house. We decided to walk to them in the late afternoon, but there was no clear way to get there. We had to cut through a few yards. Kimmie wore her 5-inch platforms and it slowed us down. When we finally got there, we sat in the middle of the last letter "O" and smoked a joint while the darkness fell all around us. The air got cool and damp and all the lights went on below us. We could see airplanes landing at the San Francisco airport, coming down over the bay....

She never ceases to amaze me. As we sat there, stoned out of our minds, she told me another puzzling and surprising thing about her private life.

She baby-sits for a mixed couple with two little boys. The Dad, Marcus, is black, and Kimmie gives him blow-jobs. He returns from his bowling game early while his skinny white wife is still out with her girlfriends. Kimmie makes sure the boys are asleep by then. She and Marcus go into his office and lock the door and she sucks his dick until tears come to her eyes. She says she has to put vaseline all over her lips because his dick is so big it feels like her mouth is going to rip at the corners.

He tried to fuck her but she's so scared it will hurt she clamps her legs together and begs him to just let her suck him off.

I say what about his wife and the children whom she has entrusted in your care???

She says, "So what?" His wife doesn't sleep with him anymore and Marcus is so nice and always gives her extra money. But she says she's not a whore he just gives her the money because he's nice. She keeps telling me she really wants me to see his dick—I won't believe how big it is.

Kimmie's parents don't seem rich but I guess they must be since they sent her to Castilleja. They are both sales representatives for some pyramid corporation, a company that sells products that clean anything and everything. We went with them to a convention once at the Cow Palace. Kimmie has all sorts of promotional products emblazoned with the company logo: bags, pencils, toothpaste, magnetic memo clips, and some withered balloons in the corner of her room.

SUNDAY, JUNE 6

I was fooled. I am at Arnie's house. I feel like I'm forcing my eyes to stay open. The right one, especially, keeps drooping closed. It's 8:20 am, and Arnie is taking a shower. I stayed overnight here. I was told there was going to be a birthday party. I even had some stupid birthday presents I got in Chinatown yesterday. However, the party consisted of only Arnie and me.

Last night, my mom drove me all the way over to Belvedere and dropped me off and left. She assumed I'd be able to get a ride home with somebody. I got there, and it was just him, and I thought I was too early and he said something like, "Yeah, I thought you might have been confused but I didn't say anything because I wasn't sure but I really wanted you to come over anyway." He was bored and lonely because his parents went bed-and-breakfasting in Sonoma for the weekend. I was so stunned. I could not believe I had gotten myself into that situation, and that I was stuck all the way across the bay with no way to get home.

Arnie ordered pizza and we ate at an elegant table that he set before my arrival. We even had wine in real wine glasses. Very fucking grown-up. When he was a small child, he told me, he dreamed of becoming a magician or a comedian. One day, a revelation came to him: "Why not be both?" *A magician that told great jokes!* What an idea!

*Arnie put on a magic
show for me,
complete with gags...*

After dinner, Arnie put on a magic show for me, complete with gags and all the equipment—a top hat, colored scarves, a Styrofoam rabbit, and trick cards. I sat and grinned with embarrassment, concealing the sadness and confusion I felt as a result of the predicament in which I had placed myself.

Then he put on a Grateful Dead album and we played darts and got quite stoned. It was getting pretty late when he asked me, "Will you have sex with me?" I never had sex offered to me in such a boldly clinical manner before. They usually just start on in and some may go as far as asking you if you mind, but since I was given the chance to give the matter a little thought, I did so, and decided against having sex with Arnie Greenwald.

We slept on bunk beds in Arnie's basement playroom.

When I was trying to fall asleep, I remembered how Arnie had a hard-on when he was talking to me at Ricky's poolside, when everyone was swimming naked. Yuk. He probably jerked off about me.

Arnie has a pasted-together personality, and if stripped of his magic show and his piano and his et cetera, he would melt and become some sort of pitiful, backboneless creature, incapable of holding conversation. He would just sit mutely quivering in some shadowed corner. He also thinks things out too completely, is too calculating. He looks like the type who, by the time they're forty, is bald and jolly looking and makes stupid jokes. He is incapable of spontaneity. He has no passion in his eyes—just a constantly questioning look.

I would never consider fucking that sneaky, weasly jerk.

I know that he and Ricky talk about me. He went so far as to admit that he asked Ricky if it would bother him if he slept with me, and of course Ricky gave him "the clear," telling him to go and do what he pleased with me. As if I would go along with it. They obviously didn't consider that perhaps I wouldn't. Before he popped the question, Arnie was giving me all these sob stories about how his 30-year-old lover (probably imaginary) had left him for an older man and how he hadn't been fucked in six months. I can't believe I walked into this trap. Birthday party!!! To top it off, the real Arnie/Ricky birthday party is next Saturday and he didn't even invite me! And I was so hurt about the whole thing, but pretended I was flattered that Arnie wanted to sleep with me, just so I wouldn't hurt his feelings.

I can't believe he could be so goddamn fucking conniving.

Here he comes. Good-bye.

MONDAY, JUNE 7

It is a cold day.

It is cold.

The Urban School faculty has discussed the matter, and decided it best that I do not return next year. I was kicked out. It seems that Minnie has been doing very little work and has completed only half the requirements necessary for the credits she had aimed at getting. My mother was really mad because my grandparents are the ones who pay my tuition and she does not want to have to explain why I have to change schools again. She says I have to tell them.

"How could you do this to me?" she said.

I offer no explanation for my failure.

The principal had asked my mother to come so he could tell us this together. He asked to talk to me for a moment without her. I had five full minutes' advance warning. He said, "If you don't tell me what's wrong, we're going to let you go. Do you understand?"

What am I going to say? The headmaster is this fat old gay guy, at least fifty, and he's obviously made up his mind he wants me out of there and nothing I could say would alter that, and my mother's outside the door and probably can hear everything. I felt trapped.

I said nothing's wrong.

He said, "You can talk to one of the other teachers if you won't talk to me." He asked me if I wanted to talk to Mr. Bill.

"No. Nothing's wrong," I said.

Maybe I'll go to Lick-Wilmerding or to public school.

I must never deny that I am responsible for the way things are. I am the navigator of my own destiny.

I am artistically talented.

I can draw well.

I can act well.

I wish there were someone neutral.

———

Monroe said maybe it's all for the best, that Urban seemed like a weird kind of school anyway, with all the rich kids and the gay principal. He said the problem is that kids in a school like Urban don't know who the boss is. And the teachers kiss the kids' asses because their jobs depend on the parents' money.

He went to high school on the Jersey Shore, somewhere near New York. He said the teachers were tough there, not a bunch of wimps like you see at these schools in California.

———

I wish my father cared whether I was dead or alive.

I never see him, never hear from him. I don't even know where he lives now. Once he called me out of the blue, and told me that my eyes were just like his, and that we know things other people can't know. He said we could see more than other people could. Like magic.

It made my grandfather sad that my Dad was not in my life much. Once my grandfather went to Bora-Bora and got me a little wooden monster carving with mother-of-pearl eyes. He told me that the spirit of my father was in it, and that I should keep it near me, and it would be just like my Dad was next to me, thinking about me, hugging me.

Magic.

WEDNESDAY, JUNE 9

Quite, quite sad. Chuck was caught hot-wiring a car, and Fred Corvin is in a mental institution. Monroe asks me, my grandfather asks me, "What do you want to do with your life?" I've done so much soul-searching between then and now, and I can only think of two things that definitely light a spark. I want to go to Africa and I want to marry Fred. I am in love with Fred. Senselessly in love. It is so frustrating. I've seen him once; I've seen him twice, no more than that. He is wild, like an animal.

My mother called Castilleja to see if I could return in the fall. But the teachers at Urban had beaten her to it. They called to ask about my past performance, and the person at Castilleja told my mother that everyone agrees that Minnie Goetze is a sneak and a liar and a bad student and would not be welcomed back at either school.

My mother called my grandparents in Philadelphia (on my father's side) and made me tell them about school. Then my mother grabbed the phone back and said that she was temporarily unemployed because she was laid off and the economy's bad and she needs more money for child support and also there will be expenses for school applications etc., etc.

Then they asked to talk to me again and my grandfather said, "Isn't your mother drinking a lot? We hear she's drinking up all the money we send."

"Of course not," I said, "she's not like that." I can't imagine who told them that, if anybody did. We live really far away and they don't know anyone we know.

The school suggested that I go to a psychiatrist.

I've felt quite sick the last few days.

I'll call Fred's mother or father tonight and ask for his phone number at the institution.

Maybe I'll knock on Fred's window. He'll come around after seeing me and open the door. I'll say, "Hi, Fred." He'll say, "Who are you?"

"Well, I went to Urban. Maybe you never saw me. It doesn't matter. I just want to say hello I just want to talk to you I just want to put my arms around you and hug you and make love to you and watch you put your motorcycle together."

I was going to go out with Chuck Saunders to a movie or something but my mother says I can't because I fucked up royally.

I love you, Fred. He stares at people's eyes, not at people, at their eyes, at their eyes, as if he were disgustedly verifying their emptiness. Fred Fred Corvin Corvin.

THURSDAY, JUNE 10

I did not go to school today. I walked down to Polk Street. There's a little candy store near the Alhambra Theatre and I bought a quarter pound of Mary Janes and a quarter pound of sour cherries. And I ate almost all of them.

I feel very sad and lonely, and the only one who can offer surcease from my sorrow is that beautiful young lesbian outside of Bob's Grill. She was so beautiful, and smiled so sweetly, I could have cried. She looked about my age. She was standing by the phone booth smoking a cigarette and I was sitting at a table inside, drinking lemonade and eating candy and writing, and she kept making eye contact. When the bus came, she threw down her cigarette and pursed her lips at me like she was blowing a kiss. Oh, my heart. Could I ever love a girl?

I feel so awkward and ugly and naive and lonely. Maybe I should kill myself maybe I should paint a picture. I always want to be touched. I don't know what's wrong with me.

It stirs up kind of a frustrated passion in my heart to think of Monroe sometimes. He hugs my mother in front of me. I don't see how he can help it—wouldn't it seem strange to her if he didn't? But when I see them I get all wracked with desire and my vision gets blurry. Both Monroe and my mom date other people but they still sleep together. I don't understand their relationship or what it means to me but I'm not allowed to talk to Monroe about it. I know I'm in no position to complain.

I have big thighs and a big ass and a big nose and I look like an R. Crumb woman.

Every time I looked up at him, his eyes rolled back and his lips parted.

I am so warm.

I want a body with mine.

I need a man.

FRIDAY, JUNE II

First there was Monroe Rutherford. He was the first. Completely.

Then there was that nameless young boy in the park. Handsome. Virile.

Thirdly, there was Ricky Wasserman, a tall, strikingly handsome classmate.

My good old friend Chuck Saunders is sitting in the next room. I can see him through a crack in the door. I told him I would have to finish typing something before I came out to play. I'm going to make him listen to my old Jackson 5 45's. I just found them. Ricky said he didn't understand why I hang out with such ugly boring creeps. Chuck is not a creep, Ricky. He is a very sensitive, thoughtful boy.

And Monroe wants to know why I let "god-fucking sneaky Jews" like Ricky Wasserman take advantage of my body. Because, Monroe, Ricky was so shamelessly attractive.

LATER

Chuck and I got really stoned and he wanted to hear "I'll Be There" again and again and he was crying like a baby. Tears just streaming down his face. He almost made me cry. After a while, hoping to lift our moods, I suggested we listen to "abc." It did cheer us up. We danced and played it again and danced some more. Then we went down to Manwell's Liquor Store and got It's Its and orange soda and Starburst fruit chews.

We all sit watching tv on the sofa. Monroe, mother, Gretel, and myself. Monroe between my mother and me. I look at his thighs, I secretly touch him. My body turns warm and blood rises to my cheek. A secret glance from his right eye... my heart pounds. I want to climb on top of his lap and put my arms around him, I want him to kiss me back and forth with his head the way he does.... It's so easy to forget that anyone else is in the room... but then the blood, the heat, drops from my head and my eyes are once more unclouded. I can see clearly once again.

SATURDAY, JUNE 12

I am seriously considering running away. My mother is constantly miserable and she's always entertaining her low-life friends. They come over and everyone sets themselves down in front of the tv and watches 'til their eyes fall out. All these friends just don't know how to amuse themselves.

Burt is stoned or else he's miserable disagreeable and hateful. He's smaller than I am but he has a glowing orb of fuzzy reddish-brown hair around his face—his head and beard are trimmed to the same longish length. He wears dark gray three-piece pinstripe suits with bell-bottom pants and expensive fag shoes and he has a pocket watch he keeps in his vest. Once I said, "Why do you have to always watch The Mary Tyler Moore Show? It's not even funny."

He got really pissed and said, "Minnie, you're always so goddamned negative. We like the show, so leave us alone and take your 24-hour downer elsewhere. Haha ha."

And Michael Cocaine is always snorting his precious powder and everyone always wants to get some from him because he's got a fantastic connection. He's got beady little black eyes and I think deep down he knows he's a fool. I know he would never snort coke around his kids but he sure feels comfortable doing it with my mom around us. It's really such a pain that my mother has all these jerks here all the time.

Mom and Andrea got some coke from Michael and it gave them the energy to clean Andrea's house all day today. Now they're here making dinner and waiting for "esquires Brad and Michael" to come over and eat and take them to Henry Africa's. They're talking about how they'll get more coke and clean our house tomorrow. They don't think I can hear them but they are very loud.

Fred, Fred, Fred, you are my only salvation, don't you see? I've got to find you.

Gretel bugs the shit out of me. She eats too much and is getting very fat. She spends all of her time watching tv in her room. It smells like garbage in there because she hides all her filthy dishes and food scraps under her bed. She doesn't want Mom to know what she's eating because she's supposed to be on a diet. She only leaves her room to go to the bathroom or to school.

She spends all her time watching TV in her room...

MONDAY, JUNE 14

Fred Corvin's mother said that he would love to hear from me. Please do call him, she pleaded. She has never heard of me, but as soon as she recognized my voice as female, she warmed up to me. "Fred needs female companionship," she said. "He is in the mental ward, third floor, at

Mount Zion Hospital on Sutter Street. The number is Jordan (JO)7-6600. Be sure to ask to be transferred to the third floor phone." She didn't know if he'd be back at school in the fall. She sounded upset. Chuck says Fred doesn't like his mother. He says he tried to kill her, which is why he's there. He heard that Fred choked her until she was unconscious.

Kimmie is going to visit him with us. She is curious.

TUESDAY, JUNE 15

We went to the mental institution, Kimmie, Chuck, and I. We got our visitors passes and took the elevator to the third floor. Patients shuffling up and down the halls. Up and down, up and down. No pianos even. No rugs on the floor, no pleasant little knick-knacks with which to amuse oneself. Not at all like Sylvia Plath. A woman with huge drooping breasts and a pink negligee scuffled down the hall. Heads bobbed up and down, up and down. People walked back and forth and back and forth. Some sat in the lounge watching TV TV TV TV TV TV TV Fred was asleep on his bed in his yellow room. He had his boots and all his clothes on. He was wrapped up tightly in a sheet, just his head peeking out. We stared at him until he felt our vibrations and opened his eyes. Oh, hi, oh hi oh hi!!

We sat around for hours. Then Chuck and I left Fred and Kimmie alone to kiss and hug. Yes, they had only just met, but Fred could not take his eyes off her! It was as if she was the first girl he had seen after years of solitary confinement. I think Fred thought that I was Chuck's girlfriend—he barely noticed me! We went to Fisherman's Wharf for a joyless look-around while they carried on behind a closed sanitarium door.

Oh, how much more jealous could I have been? Not much more, no, I think not.

I will make plans to visit Fred alone.

The guard who gave us our passes said that Fred is homicidal. "He will kill and he will feel no remorse."

I called Fred later, and he said that Kimmie told him not to fool around with me. "Why?" he asked me, "will you ask her?" I didn't understand either. I asked Kimmie. "I don't know," she said. "I just don't know...."

I will get him, though. I will get him a million times over and over again and again. Kimmie can go to hell.

He was wrapped up tightly in a sheet, just his head peeking out.

WEDNESDAY, JUNE 16

In Fred's room at the asylum, everything is blurred. I look at an object. A slipper. A panel on the wall. A face. The lines are not definite. The boundary between rose and stem seems to shift. Like a swarm of bees in magnificent form, copying nature, these objects seem strangely animated; the room seems to buzz.

He lay his head against my chest. His body followed. His heart thumping. His body so wonderfully alive, yet still. Like a package. He raised his head; he moved it back and forth, back and forth, his cheeks brushing mine, our lips touching. Our noses. His eyes looked down; they would not meet mine. Back and forth, back and forth, so delicate, so warm. Not a kiss. A touch, so warm.

A nurse walked in. "There is a man downstairs come to get you." I stood. Fred crumbled back onto his warm bed, blending into the tangle of sheets. I went downstairs.

Down the elevator. One, two, three. Three, two, one.

Monroe was waiting there. He had been talking to a nurse. "He's a killer or he will be, the doctors know. They know him. Know his type. It's too bad she has to be involved with him," the nurse told him, nodding at me. "She seems like a decent girl."

I have no feelings about any of that.

I left feeling like the center of the ocean, deep and quiet. Glowing particles of dust or old dead fish atoms slowly filter down from the top through the water. The sun gradually leaves them. They settle down later on the bottom, seven miles below. Dark. Heavy, heavy water.

THURSDAY, JUNE 17

My mother went with me to look at the public school. I cried in the car on the way home thinking about the boys in that school who steal cars and barely pass and get shit-eating jobs when they get their diplomas. I cried because there are those of them who are every bit as intelligent as Ricky Wasserman or Arnie Greenwald or Yael Berg and just because of circumstantial differences, they turn out so horribly. They see the young and affluent, they see their cars and their vacations and their fancy clothes, and they set their hearts on obtaining objects of material wealth. The young and the rich already have these things, so they are free to devote their energies to developing their minds or having good, clean fun, or anything they want, really. And they are able to set their goals on spiritual fulfillment because they have everything they need otherwise. It's just not fair. The poor ones roam the streets in their jacked-up cars and they save their money to buy slick clothes from Mervyns. They aren't allowed to realize the greater value of the intangible—the goodness of one's soul. Ricky, that fucking rich hippie, wears jeans when he can afford velvet. Those poor people—they are the ones that strive for a piece of class—they want to dress themselves well, they wear permanent-press slacks and smooth nylon printed shirts... they'd never wear jeans. The whole thing is really screwed up. As for me, I don't really care about clothes, I am in-between, not rich or poor.

I love murals. I love them more than my own self; sometimes I could just melt.

You have to live simply to survive happily. Go to school, meet a nice handsome man, marry with him and have babies. Live in the country if you can, and never send the children to public schools in the city. Love is the question and the answer.

Another letter from Pascal.

Dear Little Minnie,

I decided to write you a letter. Why? Because being an independent sort of man, I felt like it. Anyway, you're literate and I always am pleased to see your response of out-and-out placement of one word against the other. You'll never change: I suspect you will become a writer, a penniless but certainly absorbing occupation. Here goes.

Your mother and I ended our "not speaking to each other" last Saturday. You must think how dumb it is for two people to have been so passionately in love yet to have such ridiculously adolescent fallings out. Now we are cautiously courting again.

In the meantime, after having lunch with your mom, I found out that you had been only "squeaking along" at Urban and so, must find another school for the fall. Now Minnie, you are too smart to end up a dropout. And damn it, you should have called. I am, and always will be, for better or worse, your surrogate Dad. So call when things get bad. ok?

Let's stay close. We'll get it together. At least we'll try. I don't want you to have yet another father. Two's enough for anybody. Maybe we can go to the theatre, museums, and picnics. When I was growing up I had to do all that myself, good training for a publisher, but hell for feeling loved.

Anyway, I do love you. No matter what happens between your mom and me, you and Gretel will always be a part of my "family." I raised you, goddamnit.

Maybe of course you'll all return to Philadelphia. A mistake I think. But no matter, just remember that I am on your side and I love you. So that's that. Maybe I shouldn't have come out and said all this but it is in my heart. And I have so many times wanted to call you up but Mom and I were temporarily not speaking. Don't worry: we'll get it together.

Love Pascal.

LATER

Monroe sees that I get screwed by other people and that I'm not hard-up and crawling all over him. He sees that, and I think it makes him want me more... he likes it. He asks details sometimes. He says it makes me more independent but he says I shouldn't go overboard, I don't want to get jaded. And I have to learn how to choose who I go out with. Quality people, not weirdos and killers. A lot of times, I make things up, because I know he likes to hear it. He thinks I've slept with a million guys.

I like it when he kisses me in little kisses that are not just sexy... I like it when Monroe touches me tenderly, when Fred touches me tenderly, it kills me, it really does.

Monroe says to call him tomorrow morning at eight o'clock. He wants to make a plan to see me again. We want to see each other more often. I am a little bit scared... I wouldn't know what to do if he really got serious about me... this fear makes me feel all alone.

You can't disguise your youth.

Monroe looks at me and sometimes his eyes glisten softly... does he love me? I know he does... he is my good beloved friend... don't love me in more ways than that, Monroe.

Mr. Bill was kind to me today and expressed his sincere sympathy that I would have to leave the school.

I guess everyone knows. Ricky looked at me like I was a little baby, with warm eyes, smiling, sad... I almost cried.

Cloudy days are good days to love people.

FRIDAY, JUNE 18

My mother was actually nice to me today. I think she's happy because she's going to the Tubes concert tonight and the backstage party afterwards. She's going with Michael C. One of the partners at his firm knows the lead singer, Quay Lude, from high school. I wish I could go.

> *Other dudes are living in the ghetto*
> *But born in Pacific Heights don't seem much betto*
>
> *We're white punks on dope*
> *Mom and Dad moved to Hollywood*
> *Hang myself when I get enough rope*
> *I can't clean up, though I know I should*
> *White punks on dope*
> *White punks on dope*

We have one of their records. Mom promised she'd try to get Quay's autograph for me.

Monroe said he's going to take me to the Beach Boys Day on the Green concert. He just loves the Beach Boys.

That's how it all is. That sums it up and that is that.

———

Monroe told my mother that Fred is considered potentially homicidal.

Fred called me tonight. He's never called here before.

Mom answered the phone. "She's not here!" she said, as I sat clearly and certainly across the room.

"Where did she go? Who did she go out with?" he asked.

My mother said, "Minnie doesn't live here. She lives with her father and I can't give you that number."

Oh, Fred, my heart... you called me. He reminds me of a little child, he wants to cuddle... I am susceptible to children.

SATURDAY, JUNE 19

Fred asked me to be his girlfriend today. I said yes, I'd love to. He led me into the recreation room. There were people all around, and streamers, pink and blue and yellow, hanging from the ceiling and from wall to wall like

Fred said it wasn't a party for him, but I know it was.

clotheslines. The patients were playing charades. Fred said it wasn't a party for him, but I know it was. I saw a hand-painted watercolor of him, lying beside the punch. It had a signature on it and it said to Fred from so-and-so.

We went into his bedroom, and... what makes you think??!! We just kissed and hugged and he came in his pants. I wanted him to fuck me so badly....

I feel so warm. My body seems to have an overwhelming presence—I can move it any way and it moves of its own accord. My mind has no say right now in the actions of my body.

I am counting on Monroe returning from the Old Waldorf where he is with my mother having a drink so he can take me to the Mexican restaurant like he said he would. I bet he'll either forget or my mother will want to stay or some such garbage... but I want to be fucked so so badly! It just isn't fair, life.

If I don't get fucked tonight, I don't know how I'm going to get to sleep. My nerves are wracked. It's building up to something, I don't know what... if I can't get fucked....

SUNDAY, JUFNE 20

We did it in the house this morning, Monroe and I. On the couch. No one else was home. I was mad. He forgot that he was going to take me out to dinner last night. I knew he'd forget.

We did it after Mom left for the flea market with Gretel.

He's talking, or was talking, about stopping it altogether. I think he's going to get involved with my mother again. They seem to be going out more and more, and he forgets about me. I can't take it; I just can't.

What if they got married or even if he just moved in again? I don't want him to be sleeping with us both at the same time if we're living under one roof as a family. It sounds crazy, but what if he started sleeping with Gretel, too?

But today I fucked him. He's so sweet. I hope he's forgotten about discontinuing the whole thing. We had a long, meaningful talk about his self and my own self and how outside influences relate to our lives and how one must learn to utilize these influences to have them working for you, not against you. I listened attentively, and agreed. I must look out for myself. I've got to think more about how the things I involve myself with will ultimately affect me.

Monroe wants me to be more responsible and go to Planned Parenthood. Perhaps I will on Tuesday—it's teen clinic day.

You should only fuck people you love.

I wonder if I could ever fuck my own father.

I used to have dreams about my grandfather and me. We were both nude, but I'd look down, and there was nothing between his legs....

I had a dream the other night about eating avocados, so many millions of avocados. I was overwhelmed and I woke up immediately and threw up and up and up....

MONDAY, JUNE 21

Today is the first official day of summer. They play that song "Philadelphia Freedom" on the radio constantly now, because it's almost the Bicentennial. It's an awful song and it's embarrassing to me in particular because I was born in Philadelphia.

TUESDAY, JUNE 22

Today was supposed to have been my last day at the Urban School. I didn't even go. It's too unspeakably sad not to be allowed to be a part of something anymore. Even if I didn't like it in the first place.

Kimmie 'n me went to teen clinic at Planned Parenthood. We were there for hours but it was worth the wait I suppose because we got a lot of stuff for free. I got pills and a diaphragm and diaphragm jelly and a bunch of different rubbers and some foam and lots of pamphlets.

Afterwards, we went to a really cheap Chinese restaurant on Polk Street, Shin-Wah. I had a big plate of sweet and sour shrimp and Kimmie ordered tomato beef chow mein.

I had a big plate of sweet and sour shrimp.

We were the only customers and the fat waiter paid a lot of attention to us. He gave us each a bamboo calendar that said "Year of the Dragon" and "Shin-Wah," with their phone number and address below. At the top was a picture of a red and green dragon. The calendars roll up and you secure the roll with little red ties. And he gave us something like five or six fortune cookies apiece.

I would recommend this restaurant.

WEDNESDAY, JUNE 23

I'll never get to sleep with Fred. I'll never see him again. In a way, it's a relief.

He attacked one of the nurses at Mt. Zion and they transferred him to Vacaville, to some kind of mental institution/prison.

Chuck said he smashed a potted plant on the nurse's head when she went into his room to give him his medication. He ripped her clothes and pushed her under his bed. He wouldn't let anyone in his room to help her—he held her hostage somehow. Maybe he threatened to kill her. He said he wanted to be released. The police finally got him by coming in through an outside window. The nurse isn't dead, but some of the bones around her eye were smashed, and she was unconscious. I wonder if she was one of the nurses I met there. I remember a really pretty one with long blond hair.

Chuck says that Fred will probably be in Vacaville for years.

It really is so hard to believe that I was so close to really getting involved with him. It's so sad. I wonder what made him that way?

Even Chuck has second thoughts about calling Fred now after what happened, even though they were best friends.

I am definitely tired of my emotionless sex life.

I got fucked by Ricky today. It was weird. He was in San Francisco, so he called and he said he wanted to talk. He came to my house and met my mom briefly, then we went to Julius Kahn Park and walked around. Of course, we couldn't really talk we just fucked. Not only do I no longer feel a damn thing in my heart for the dear boy, but it was also the worst fuck I have ever had.

Later, my mom said she thought he wasn't as cute as I said he was. She said he looks skinny, but he's got a flabby ass. And she didn't think he was very polite.

I was also fucked by Monroe. Substantially better, but only slight physical titillations. I suppose today was just not my day. I was simply socially uninspired.

Monroe nags me about how I'm going to grow up to be sexually jaded. What the hell does "jaded" mean? I'm going to have had too much too soon and I'm not going to be able to have any fulfilling sexual-emotional relationships with anyone because I take sex too lightly, too impersonally. He should tell me now! He always acts like he wants me to fuck everybody, and we were hardly in love when this whole thing started!

For the past week, I have been growing paler and there are circles under my eyes. I think tomorrow I will go sit under the sky.

Monroe is on the couch, sleeping.

THURSDAY, JUNE 24

Last night I called Cosmic Conference about a million times and finally got through. There was some creepy person named McCarty making quiet pained animal noises, and a bunch of other idiots, mostly guys. I was feeling rather eloquent and was saying some pretty clever things, I thought, amusing myself at least, and someone named Robert gave me another number to call to talk to him alone... I called him and he said that he owns Cosmo. I didn't tell him who I really am, because how can I know if he's telling the truth?

LATER

How does one become a prostitute? Go down to Market Street until you see a tall, thin black man with high-heel boots and a cape and a big hat and a diamond in his lapel.

Then you give him the eye, you know, and just hope that he takes it from there. Of course if you so display your boldness, he may not want you because he assumes that you'd be really uncool and perhaps blow his cover. And besides, how can he be sure that you're not a cop? It's not often that someone actually just steps up out of the blue and offers to be a whore. And also, what if the guy's not even a pimp?

What is one to do?

You could go to Nevada and get a job in some cheap brothel, then take it from there and somehow get back to the streets of San Francisco... but I'd

How does one become a prostitute?

have to be really good at whatever I was expected to do. Maybe they have men who teach you. And I'd have to be pretty, but I'm not so I'd probably get a bad job. You don't get any money from being a plain old slut.

SATURDAY, JUNE 26

I have gone to bed with someone every day for the past four. Tuesday, it was Monroe. Wednesday, Monroe and Ricky. Thursday, Monroe, and Friday, Ricky. I wonder if I can keep it up. I've sure been getting fucked a lot lately.

I went to a graduation party last night and this morning. Ricky and I borrowed a car for a while. I thought I'd never see him again, but Jill called me up and invited me. He was wearing brown pants, a black vest, and a frilly light blue shirt. I decided to experiment a little. I panted and breathed hard hard hard and kissed him all over while he was fucking me. I made lots of little noises... it was fun. He said that it really freaked him out that I was so responsive. He said I had a real talent in the sack, and that it was just about the best fuck he had ever had. What a nice thing for him to say.

I inhaled a lot of amyl nitrate. A whole, whole lot. And I got very drunk. A bunch of black guys in the band kept trying to pick up on me, but I told them I had a broken leg so I couldn't go anywhere. I developed a convincing limp. After a while, I began to get very obnoxious. I cried and cried... all over Susan and Amy and Steve and Kathy and everyone else.... Ricky got mad, but Chuck was very wonderful to me in my time of need. I was crying about Ricky and I told them how I felt bad because I had been taken advantage of by so many people—Fred and Ricky and Kurt and Monroe.... Of course, I was exaggerating, but it sounded pretty good.

Fun fun fun. I deserted Chuck and Kimmie, the ones who brought me, so they went back to San Francisco without me. I left the party at two and got to Amy's house about three... I called home but no one answered, so I called Monroe and told him to call my mother and tell her where I was. But he forgot or something and my mother was furious this morning. She didn't know where I was and got so worried that she didn't go to the flea market. Instead, she and Kimmie sat and called all of my friends... except Amy, of course. Chuck said that maybe I had killed myself because last night I had casually listed suicide among my options. So, my mother had a huge crying jag, and then Monroe calls her and tells her where I am. She made me clean the whole house and the car today. She and Gretel and Monroe went to the beach.

I do enjoy music.

I have so much energy. It's literally coming off my body as steam. I am always hot and my heart is always pounding faster than is the usual.

Summer thoughts

Summer Vacation

Carefree adventure
with change lurking
in the wings.

———

My first comic: It's just one page, but it took me a really long time to do.

Monroe was here today, appearing unusually pale and wan. His shoulders drooped when he wasn't sitting, which was only rarely since he was feeling rather rheumy.

I thought he was joking, which is something he more than often does. But he wasn't. He went to two hospitals and he has to go to a urologist tomorrow. Bloody pee bloody pee. I almost had a heart attack when I realized he wasn't lying. I hope he doesn't die. I don't want to sleep. My mom is letting him stay at our house tonight, thank God. I am truly worried. Pray.

I paint my toenails nowadays. I stole the colors—dark brown-red, red-red, purple, and shimmering pearly pink-red. They are all from Woolworth's on Polk Street.

MONDAY, JUNE 28

I finished my first comic. It's just one page, but it took me a really long time to do. It's about walking around the city. I used India ink but I have no idea what kind of paper you're supposed to use or what kind of pen point. I got a bunch of different crow-quill nibs at Flax.

I want to discipline myself to draw and write every single day.

I think if I ever were a real cartoonist, I wouldn't be interested in just being funny. In fact, very few cartoons amuse me. I hate most cartoons.

———

Monroe just left. It's 3:00. He's got a doctor's appointment at 4:00. He stayed overnight, in my mom's room, but he said they didn't do anything. How could he have, in his condition? He left this morning but came back later to give me something to type. No one else was home so then of course he starts brushing up against me and playfully punching me in the arm and I say quit it what about your disorder or disease or whatever and he says it's not so bad and he unzips his pants like I'm going to suck his dick or something no way I said and I pushed him on the couch and got on top of him and you know what, but I just went really slowly so he wouldn't be further injured.

Maybe he's not really sick.

I am nearing the point of accepting myself as I truly am. I feel I have a reasonable inner picture of my body, and I'm no longer uncomfortable with its appearance. Not because I think it's particularly beautiful, but because it's regular and besides, I don't give a damn about how I look anymore. At least not today.

Monroe said that he might take me up to the high Sierras to go fishing in a deep-flowing stream on Saturday. He asked me if I would still want to go even if the doctor says he's not able to "perform" because of his kidney and all. Of course I'd still go. I'd mind a little though. Not too much.

I am thinking seriously about becoming a bartender when I grow up. Monroe and my mother got more depressed when I asked them for their opinions.

TUESDAY, JUNE 29

Monroe says he can't go fishing because he has to work on his mailings for his athletic nutritional supplements. And he forgot to get tickets for the Beach Boys. I don't like him as much as I did before his illness.

Pascal called and said doodling away at comics may be ok for now, but I've got to think about more serious things like writing.

———

I wrote a fan letter to Aline Kominsky.

WEDNESDAY, JUNE 30

Minnie's Favorite Things (as of June)

Favorite Color: Purple.

Favorite Song: "Memory Motel" by the Rolling Stones, or "House of the Rising Sun" by the Animals. Or "Gathering Flowers for the Master's Bouquet" by Kitty Wells. "Apartment Number 9" by Tammy Wynette or "Ball and Chain" by Janis Joplin.

Favorite Food: Eggs.

Favorite Book: *Demian* or *The Princess and the Goblin* or *Soul on Ice* or *Women in Love* or....

Favorite Movie: *Virgin Spring* by Ingmar Bergman.

Favorite Person: Monroe or Daddy or PopPop... oh, it's so unfair... I really feel washed out by everyone.

Favorite Artist: R. Crumb or Heironymous Bosch or Aline Kominsky (The Bunch) or Diane Noomin (Didi Glitz) or Justin Green (Binky Brown) or Van Eyck or Peter Paul Rubens, especially that huge *Prometheus Bound* painting in the Philadelphia Museum of Art.

What do you want to be?: An art museum curator or just a plain artist or a bartender. Or perhaps a taxidermist or a mortician. Or a speleologist. A serious, intellectual type... a muralist... a cartoonist (*not* the newspaper kind)... oh, god, anything.

Didi Glitz is one of my favorite characters.

I went to the beach and got sunburned and tanned. Monroe is here now to take Gretel and me to the flicks. I wish she wasn't going but it's all in the name of normalcy.

THURSDAY, JULY 1

I went to a comic book publishing company today. I called and asked how a person could get their comics published, and they said if I live in San Francisco I could just take the bus to Bryant Street and show my stuff to them in person, even if it wasn't ready for publication. I didn't think about it too long—I just went. I got there just before 5:00 and met the owner, a big fat hippie with a long beard and smiling eyes, and he looked at my stuff and said if I wanted to be a cartoonist, I'd have to learn how to draw everything, cars and fire hydrants and all different animals. He showed me original art by Crumb, Spain, and Bill Griffith. He picked up one of Crumb's pages, and closing his eyes, he moved his hand slowly over the surface of the paper. "You can feel the drawing... you can feel the bump of the dried ink, the blobs and traces..." He loved the art. He let me feel it, too.

He didn't say if he liked my comics or anything—he looked at them for a long time and then just started giving me advice. One thing that was strange—he was wearing really short cut-offs and when I was sitting next to him on the beat-up couch in his office I swear I could see the tip of his dick sticking out from beneath the leg of his shorts. I tried not to look.

Then he took me into the warehouse and some of the workers showed me all the comics, stacks and stacks of them on shelves on the wall, and they gave me whatever I wanted. I came home with about twenty-five new books. I'm going to read them tonight. Two look great: *Amputee Love* and *White Whore*.

Amputee Love is pretty unusual.

FRIDAY, JULY 2

Today I was walking around North Beach by myself... I was thinking about dropping in on Monroe. I wanted to but I felt sort of shy... I was just walking around, looking at things, and I passed this little restaurant, Golden Boy Pizza, which I'm sure I passed six million times before. The figure of a boy was painted on the window above the name of the restaurant, and I stood on the sidewalk staring at it because it was familiar in a way I couldn't place. Suddenly, I realized that Justin Green had painted it! He's the one who does *Binky Brown Meets the Holy Virgin Mary*. Even though his name wasn't on the window, I know he did it—it was unmistakably his style. I was so excited that I wanted to tell someone about it. But I really don't have any friends who are even remotely interested in comics. So I told an old lady that was struggling up the hill on a cane. She smiled at me as she passed, so I smiled back and blurted out, "I know the guy who painted this sign!" I know I lied but I didn't want to explain all about comics. The lady said it was a very nice picture.

Then I went to Caffe Trieste and got seltzer water with mint syrup and I sat there and drew for awhile instead of going to Monroe's house.

I'm baby-sitting tonight for the Golds, who live a block away on Walnut Street. Ms. Gold is an actress and is a foot taller than Mr. Gold, who I've only seen in a business suit. They have two daughters, three and ten. The youngest is hyperactive and the ten-year-old is a precocious brat. Ms. Gold has a silkscreen portrait of herself made by Andy Warhol. I like looking at their stuff.

White Whore is funny.

SATURDAY, JULY 3

Kimmie and me are going out today to meet Marcus, the black guy she baby-sits for... she wants us both to fuck him. She says she always talks about me because I'm her best friend and Marcus said he'd like to meet me. And now they've made this plan where we meet and go to some hotel.

Oh my god Oh my god ohmygod

It is a quarter to two in the afternoon and I have just finished making and eating a fried egg. I am now enjoying a hot cup of instant Suisse Mocha. My mind is all a-jumble. My mom had a party last night. Andrea was there, and Nancy O'Flanigan, and Michael C., and all these other lawyer guys, and some people I didn't know. And Kimmie and Monroe. People were snorting coke in Mom's bedroom and we tried to go in there too but people kept shooing us away. Later, no one cared what we did. Kimmie and I and probably everyone else got totally stoned on Burt Allen's pot. Nancy O'Flanigan brought her British exchange student, Ian (nineteen), and he brought a bunch of Pink Floyd albums that he played at full volume. He is very serious about music and hardly said a word to anyone. He was content to look through all our records and play dj.

Burt sat at her feet holding a microphone...

Later on, after midnight, only four or five people were left, and we all sat around in my mother's room. It was Burt and Monroe and my mother and I along with the cognac and the sherry and the marijuana. The coke was all gone. Kimmie was fast asleep on the couch.

Mom played the guitar, the same song over and over again,

Freight train, freight train, run so fast,
Freight train freight train run so fast,
Please don't tell what train I'm on
They won't know what route I'm going.
When I'm dead and in my grave
No more good times here I crave
Place the stones at my head and feet
And tell them all that I've gone to sleep

...No wait, no wait, let me start again...

Burt sat at her feet holding a microphone, staring up at her with glazed eyes, recording the song. The way she sings it sounds so lost and wistful, like a pitiable child looking for a home, scared of everything, and just running until it dies.

Monroe and I went to the kitchen to eat eggs and soon we were caught up in a passionate embrace. We scrambled five eggs and made French toast of the rest. We kissed with crumbs in our mouths while the butter burned. Mom and Burt had fallen asleep while waiting for their eggs. Everyone loves eggs.

We stumbled down the back stairs to the basement and made love by the washer and dryer. I cannot tell you how passionate, like waves, hot moist breath... I kissed it and sucked it and then he lay on top of me under the ping-pong table I could feel the throbbing inside of me when he came I love it with him he is so hot he is such a big man some women don't like men with hairy chests I wonder how they couldn't. I want to do it again. When we went upstairs Burt was in the kitchen stumbling around. He seemed surprised to see us together. He mumbled something about how he thought I was asleep. We said we had been downstairs looking for the cat.

I went to Paradise. To visit Kimmie's cousin Doreen and her husband and kids. I was there three long days, with Kimmie and her mother. It's near Sacramento. The whole trip driving up there, we sang two songs over and over again: "Memory Motel" and "Mercedes Benz." We were practicing our country singing voices.

Kimmie was obsessed with the idea of fucking Doreen's husband. She finally did but it didn't go over very well because Doreen became suspicious even though Kimmie and Jay denied doing anything.

We were stoned for the whole trip and the tension was high. I felt constantly worried and paranoid. I tried to stay in our room and read because I didn't want to talk to anybody because I knew what was going on.

At one point, while Kimmie's mom and Doreen and her kids were out shopping, Kimmie kicked me out of the room so she could fuck Jay again.

It was so fucking hot. I was wearing one of Kimmie's bathing suits and her shoes and spent an hour wandering around the rest of the house touching things and looking at things and hoping no one came home.

I was wearing one of Kimmie's bathing suits.

The next day we went shooting at a rifle range in Martinez but I did not want to shoot, especially with Kimmie's low-life cousins who terrified me, so I sat in the snack bar area reading and pretending not to notice all the creepy white-trash rifle men staring at me.

LATER

Dear Confidante,

I really don't know how Kimmie feels about me. She sure hangs around me a lot. I told her that I thought our friendship was shallow, not really deep-rooted, and that it wasn't really satisfying to me because we never talk.

"What do you mean, we never talk? We talk all the time!"

"We just never talk about anything deep, you know."

"No. I don't know. What are you talking about?"

I told her I felt trapped, with no room to grow. Kimmie got mad and hurt and said she didn't know what I was talking about and that she didn't want to discuss it anymore.

I can't expand because she won't let her mind expand with mine. I feel like I'm dragging her around like a dead weight. She's intelligent, but I think more than she does. About different things, maybe. She's good company and has a practical head but she just doesn't understand me. Lots of people don't understand me. They always have reasons for things and expect me to have reasons, too. I'm impulsive. I don't always give a lot of thought to the things I do or say. It must seem like I'm insensitive to others' feelings... but I'm not. It's just that nobody understands me.

I guess, in fact, that I did something incomprehensible just the other day. I gathered together all the means of birth control I got at the Teen Clinic and I put everything into my backpack. I walked over to California Street and dumped it all into a public trashcan, away from my house. It just gave me a sick feeling to think of rubber in my belly and cream inside of me and synthetic hormones invading my blood stream.

SATURDAY, JULY 10

I think I am in love with Monroe. He is at EST for two days and then he goes to New York for a week, so I probably won't see him until the week after. It seems like such a long time. He left when I was in Paradise. When I awoke this morning and realized that he was gone, I felt so sad... I miss him too much to call what I feel just a passing fancy. I feel protective of him. I don't want anyone to hurt him or think badly of him. I worry about his kidneys and I hate it when he has to drive home in the middle of the night when he's been drinking. I hate it when he has to drive home, period.

I wish I could see him more often without having to be so secretive about it. It's not fair that we have to be undercover with our relationship. Sometimes I feel like telling my mom and risk suffering the consequences.

What would she do if she knew?

Maybe she would turn on me and hate me and never let me see Monroe again. Then I'd have no one. Or maybe she'd have him arrested and she'd realize I need care and she'd love me like never before.

I hate everything. I hate clinics, I hate medicine, and I hate Monroe's job. I wish he lived in a sailboat. I wish I were with him. I wish he didn't always talk about my mother. I wish my mother had a job.

Andrea told me that some people say EST is a cult that brainwashes people and tries to intimidate them by controlling them. She's heard stories that they say things to try to make people cry, and you can't go to the bathroom unless they give you permission.

SUNDAY, JULY 11

Kimmie slept over last night. We took about ten of Mom's old albums to Rooks and Becords on Polk street and a guy named Scott, a chubby desk clerk who's always nice to us, helped us trade them in for the best David Bowie records he had on hand. We really wanted them because we both love that song ch-ch-ch-changes.

Scott said, "You know that Commodores song Brick House? You know what it means? It means that the girl is really well built, like a brick shithouse. That's what it really is. And you two are built like a couple of brick shithouses." He was trying to flatter us but we were disgusted. I'm sorry, but no matter how you look at it, it sounds like some sort of twisted put-down to call someone a "shithouse."

We went back to my house and listened to *ch–ch–ch–ch–ch–ch–ch–ch–changes* about a hundred times and now we both definitely love Bowie even more. We kept looking at the pictures on the albums trying to figure out if he was cute or not, but all the pictures were really too small or he had too much makeup on to tell for sure. There's one picture on the front of the David Live album where he's wearing a blue suit and Kimmie said, "Look at me!" right before our favorite part of the song, the first time he says "ch-ch-ch..." and then, right when he says it, she starts licking the crotch of the picture. "You try it too," she says, "just lick his dick, right through his pants—try it! It really feels likes there's something there!"

I tried it, and it's true—if you close your eyes and lick the right spot, you feel this little tiny dick, about half an inch long, and hard as a rock. Ha!

I guess Kimmie's ok... we have fun sometimes.

MONDAY, JULY 12

I got a postcard from Aline Kominsky today. She said she never got a letter from a girl before, just from greasy fan-boys who think she's cute. Now I feel even more inspired to draw.

I got a postcard from Aline Kominsky today.

TUESDAY, JULY 13

Mom's friend Martin Chong took me to dinner at La Pantera and then to play air hockey at an arcade on Broadway in North Beach. He knew that I was interested in cartooning and he wanted to talk. He said that he loved comics when he was a kid, and he tried to draw, but he wasn't much good at it. He's a lawyer now, but he still keeps a collection of old Donald Duck and Superman comics.

I showed him the postcard I got from Aline and he was really impressed and excited.

He was interested in my artwork and he said he thought I was very talented and he wanted me to draw him in pen and ink someday, maybe tomorrow. We went to City Lights on Columbus, because he wanted to buy a book he could only get there. He bought me two comics: Arcade 2 and 4.

I was sure his motive was to put the moves on me. But he didn't. Maybe he was trying to be fatherly or big brotherly. Maybe he's just trying to get closer to my mother through me. I know he has a crush on her.

He's the one who wrote:

> Waiting and hoping for thy step,
> Sleepless in bed I lie,
> All through the night, until the moon,
> Leaving her post on high,
> Slips sideways down the sky.

WEDNESDAY, JULY 14

Monroe called me last night at twenty to three all the way from New Jersey. He called to tell me all about how he got arrested for drunk driving and not wearing any shoes or having his wallet in the car. The policeman was really nice to him and let him ride around in the police car, chasing criminals, until Monroe sobered up. Monroe said I was the only one who would appreciate a story like that.

Then he let me talk to some girl named Rhonda and she told me the whole story as it really was—and it wasn't much different—but I found out that his shoes were on the front doorstep all the time, but no one could figure out where Monroe was. Rhonda was really nice. She said that Monroe must really love me because he's always talking about me. When she said that my heart nearly stopped and I couldn't breathe for a moment. I didn't tell her I was fifteen. I wondered if she thought I was my mother.

Monroe calls me sometimes in the middle of the night when he is drunk. I pull the phone into my room at night just in case he calls. Otherwise my mother answers and he talks to her instead. I really like it because the nighttime when he's drunk is when he gets all unsecret and tells me how much he wants me. Just last night he told me he really missed me and when could we get together again—immediately? I'm going to see him the day he gets back. Sunday.

I really miss him and I can't wait until he's here again. I love Monroe. Sometimes I watch him as he sleeps, and I feel so much love for him that

Sometimes I watch him as he sleeps, and I feel so much love for him.

my heart feels like it might burst. I wish that the minute he comes off the plane I could run up to him and hug him tight. But I can't, darnit, because my mother will be there. It's just not right that we have to hide our affection. Do you think it's right? Or do you think that Monroe is just some old lecher who is taking advantage of me? And if he's not taking advantage of me, do you think it's a horrible sin all the same? I wish Monroe had a diary so you could read both sides of the situation and tell me what's what.

———

Just because he kept asking me, I finally told Monroe that Kimmie and I fucked Marcus, even though it's not true.

"Jesus, you really like to fuck, don't you?" he said. His voice was slurry. "And what about that Kimmie? She really likes to fuck too, doesn't she? What am I gonna do with you girls?"

FRIDAY, JULY 16

I worked diligently on a comic most of the week.

I was bored this evening so I called Cosmo. Nobody was on it, just a couple of guys talking about a baseball game. I didn't say anything. I just listened to their conversation while I drew a picture. Someone else called in later, and I recognized his voice as Robert, the overseer. I just said "hi," and he recognized my voice immediately and asked me to call him back on his home phone. I did.

He runs the whole thing out of his basement in a house near the Cow Palace where he lives with his parents, but he says he's moving out as soon as he can find a good place for himself. He's 24 and he just finished a certificate in engineering or electronics at City College. He says Cosmo is just a little black box. He makes tapes of the conversations. It's a hobby, and he feels like a spider waiting for flies to come along... he listens to them... there are all sorts—mostly young, but some he can't tell their age, some pretend to be other people, some are nuts, some are just trying to pick up girls... it's all there, he says, and it's fascinating. He said maybe he'd play some tapes for me if I were curious. He said I was one of the more interesting girls who calls Cosmo, and he knows my voice even when I disguise it. He knows who Kimmie is too, but he was more interested in me.

I hate Coca-Cola. I like grape soda, orange soda, and cream soda.

I really like candy.

Candy that I like.

My favorite kinds of candy are: Junior Mints, Bit-o-Honey, Abba Zabba, and Good & Plenty.

SATURDAY, JULY 17

Dear Minnie,

Remember? Today was the day you went with your mother to the airport to pick up Monroe Rutherford, the dashing thirty-five-year-old blonde with whom you are having an affair, who incidentally is one of your mother's lovers. Remember? He had just arrived home from a week on the East Coast and, as your mother explained to him that she was going out to lunch with Martin Chong, he suggested that you and he go down to the Alameda Marina to check out the sailboats. So you went, and decided that deep navy blue made even the cheapest boats look dignified. Then you both went to McDonald's. And then and then and then you went to his apartment with him and had sexual intercourse and fell asleep for an hour then woke up and went home and Monroe went out to dinner with your mother and now you are supposed to be cleaning your room, but instead you are typing this document of the day's events. Remember?

Yes, I remember.

Although it's not very vivid in my mind any longer.

Sometimes I actually wish that I had never gotten involved with Monroe. I can never see him often enough or when I feel I really need to. And the whole situation is so sneaky that sometimes I am disgusted. And I feel like such a child, so intellectually, physically, and emotionally inferior to his stupid friends even though they happen to be a bunch of fucking bores....

I would like to own someone. I would like to be able to look at a man and think, "He's mine, and no one else can touch him and he can touch no one but me."

"Oh, hee hee hee, look! It fits my big toe!"

Yesterday, Monroe took Kimmie Minter, my best friend, and me to Bolinas with him. Kimmie was still sort of cold to me because of what I said about our friendship. She was pissed off and she called me a snob. I told her I guess I had just been in a weird mood.

We played around on the beach for a while. We were the only ones there. The sky was gray, more to the blue side of gray with a tinge of rosy pink. The water was dark. It was smooth and nearly waveless. There was energy in the air as if before a storm.

We sat in the sand, leaning against a dune. We each drank a couple beers and then decided to go to Monroe's apartment. Kimmie and I kissed in the car. We touched each other's breasts. We took a bath at his house. Oh, how can I explain this—it gets me sick it is so pornographic. To Kimmie it was just another casual encounter. She's always either stupidly infatuated with a guy or else she doesn't care and it's just another fuck. I don't want people to think of Monroe that way. I don't like other people not to care about him because I love him. But Kimmie just chalked it up under "new experiences," and that was that. There is nothing truly passionate about her. The sexual nature of Kimmie Minter is a viscous cervical mucus that *always* welcomes mating. She was slimy and wet even though she always says she doesn't like Monroe and she says Marcus' dick is much bigger and it's too bad I didn't see it.

He fucked both of us and he came inside both of us and we jumped around and sang to the Beach Boys while we waited for him to rest so he could get it up again. We both sucked his cock and he ate us out and we ate each other out and we all moaned and groaned and beer was spilled and Kimmie threw up on the bed while Monroe and I took one last bath together.

Kimmie is the epitome of all I don't like in myself. That's why I can understand her. She flirts and she lusts only for the physical aspects of sex. She acts dumb in front of men and is constantly begging for attention. She's always trying to be cute. She tried Monroe's graduation ring on her big toe since it didn't fit any of her fingers. "Oh, hee hee hee, look! It fits my big toe!" she giggled. She's always doing cute things like that. Monroe didn't like it one bit and told her to get the ring the fuck off her foot and give it back to him.

She tries, she really tries. She wants to appear innocent. That's how she charms the idiots and long string of Italians and Chicanos and old men and black guys she's added to her list. But Monroe is wise to her act. Unfortunately, he, too, is now just another name on her list, and so am I—I'm her first girl.

I better stop typing. Kimmie's almost out of the shower.

WEDNESDAY, JULY 21

My friend Elizabeth, from Castilleja, came to visit for a few days.

Monroe is going to take us to the Boardinghouse to hear some "country rock" with Gretel and a woman named Karyn. She's a secretary for an executive in some big company.

Monroe used to date Karyn before he dated my mother. Monroe said she just called him up out of the blue last week for old time's sake. He says she's always wanted more from him than he's willing to give. He said she's too straight-laced and mid-western for his tastes.

I think he's letting us tag along because he doesn't want to be alone with her.

THURSDAY, JULY 22

Karyn seemed surprised that Monroe had invited us to go out with them.
She was really tall and skinny and all dolled up with jewelry and a lot of
perfume. She was pretty but she just didn't have any spark. She seemed
really straight. I can see why she bugs Monroe. But it's obvious that *she's*
in love with *him*.

She glared at us the whole time at the nightclub because Monroe kept
ordering pitchers of beer and Elizabeth and I were drinking it like fish.
Gretel had a couple of Shirley Temples. Elizabeth got very drunk and threw
up in the car on the way home. The vomit was bright orange because we
had been eating Cheeze Puffs.

Karyn was furious and shocked and disgusted and got out of the car at
Lombard and Van Ness and walked home alone to her efficiency apartment
in the Marina. Gretel started crying so we drove her home.

Then we drove back to Monroe's house so Elizabeth could clean the
vomit off her body and my mom wouldn't find out. Gretel called to see what
was taking us so long and we told her that Elizabeth had passed out and
that we would have to spend the night at Monroe's house. But of course,

that wasn't entirely the truth. We could have easily come home but Monroe and me were kind of drunk too. We all got into the same bed and Monroe and I made love all night while Elizabeth lay beside us making drunken comments like what does it feel like? She kept wanting just to look at Monroe's dick. She's a virgin and Monroe kept saying shouldn't I fuck her too? He probably thinks that since he fucked Kimmie, he can fuck all of my friends. I made him leave her alone. We fell asleep at the break of dawn.

FRIDAY, JULY 23

Elizabeth went home this afternoon. She had lunch with Pascal and then he drove her to the airport because he's a friend of Elizabeth's parents—that's why I went to Castilleja. They said it was such a great school. Elizabeth lives in Pacific Palisades, near la, I think.

It's kind of irritating, however, the way that Pascal seems to compare Elizabeth to me. Not outright, exactly, but he's always saying that she's a brilliant student etc. etc., and of course I clearly am not.

I told Kimmie that Elizabeth and I went out with Monroe etc. etc. and she laughed so hard and said I should have let Monroe fuck Elizabeth!

"She's such a prude and she's so shy! She needs it!"

SATURDAY, JULY 24

Mom took me to The Palms, a club on Polk Street, because R. Crumb's band, The Cheap Suit Serenaders, was playing there. It was very spur-of-the-moment. Of course I was happy but scared to meet him. I was hoping Aline would be there, but she wasn't. My mother really likes the kind of music they play. I don't know what you call it—it's kind of old-timey, tinny banjo music. Mom ordered about five gin and tonics and I probably drank the equivalent of two because she let me take as many sips of hers as I wanted.

During the intermission, Mom went up to the stage and said to Crumb, "My daughter got a letter from your girlfriend!"

He immediately knew who I was and even remembered my name! I wanted to tell him something, I mean, nothing specific, just *something*, but it was too hard because I felt so shy around him. He probably thought I was just some silly fan.

Mom was very "on," and she made friends with a few of the guys in the band. One of them works in the unemployment office so she's going to look for him next time she has to get her check, and she gave her phone number to another one because he said he could teach her to play mandolin. He's a cartoonist too. I saw his stuff in *Arcade*. I like it. He does *Mickey Rat*.

Monroe was not impressed that we met R. Crumb. He says, "I liked that kind of shit, those head comics, when I was in college. I can't believe Art Crumb is still around! Is he still doing those comics? Does anyone *read* that stuff anymore? He must be kind of an old guy, isn't he?"

SUNDAY, JULY 25

Chuck called. His parents kicked him out and now he's living with his twenty-five-year-old brother in Pacifica. His brother's wife is very uptight about Chuck. He doesn't really like living there.

He's going to become an emancipated minor and take the ged so he can start working and not go to school. He definitely doesn't want to go back to Urban. He sounded totally high. Where is Pacifica?

Chuck was really psyched. He's making a lot of money because he's got two vials of acid, which is about a million hits. He makes up sheets of blotter. He said maybe he'd come over one day and I could help him cut it up into hits.

TUESDAY, JULY 27

Last night I had a dream that my mother was looking for me. Her face was red and anxious and she was pulling a tall, gray-suited man by the hand. They found me in a long hallway and told me they knew about Monroe. My mother said that she had really known all along but she had never mentioned it because she didn't want to embarrass anyone. She said that she wasn't mad. She was just worried, so she had brought along the nice psychiatrist. He asked me the kind of questions I love to answer, interesting questions about my deepest self, while my mother listened to my replies. He asked me if I had been sad and if I had loved Monroe or still did. He asked me what I thought should be done. He sounded like he genuinely cared about me, and my mother seemed to have all her hope and trust endowed in him.

I think I dreamed that dream because last night I was talking to Monroe outside my mother's bedroom door just after she had gone to sleep. He was talking regularly but I was whispering and it bothered me that he didn't lower his voice.

I was terribly upset last night. I had cleaned the kitchen thoroughly and my mother had promised that I could go with Monroe and her to look at a boat Monroe was thinking of getting. But Monroe said no, I couldn't go. My mother usually doesn't want to go so I do. They probably went to fuck. It is all of little importance. Anyway, I went into my room and cried desperately for a short time, then stiffened my upper lip and wiped away my tears and sneaked a beer into my purse (I was already inebriated from the two glasses of wine I had at dinner).

I told everyone I was going to visit Tisha Shelley, a girl I used to know from Castilleja. Instead, I took a 55 down to Chinatown. I was going to get off at Polk, but something stopped me. It was lucky that I got off where I did, at Grant Street, because I met a man, George Dunn, an old man, about seventy, who was once a gardener in Golden Gate Park. We walked through Chinatown together and stopped at the coffee shop he always goes to (the kind that has both Chinese and American baked goods) and ate pie and talked for a long time....

He poured out his philosophy of life to me, and made me more aware of my possibilities as a person. He made me realize that a person is self-made, and that one may either accept or reject any influences on one's personality. He taught me that I had to grow and learn my aspirations, realizing that I can never reach perfection on Earth, but that I should try to be humble and loving and understanding and divinely sweet and of good will because I had potential as a good, happy, and friendly person because I am sensitive.

He said that women are God's most perfect creation because they are more heart than mind and less cold and more understanding and because they have intuition, which is a godly type of understanding. He told me that it is a sin to live a useless, empty life and that I should do what I can with what I've got and not be pretentious and that I should stay pure and bright and innocent in my own mind. He said that the ultimate goal of marriage should be to bear children, and that if someone doesn't plan to have children, they shouldn't marry, unless they're old and it's more for companionship anyway.

"Your purity and innocence shine through," he said. "Keep your angel eyes." I blushed and looked away.

"Everyone has bad thoughts," he said, "it's only human."

"Everyone has bad thoughts."

"There are very few bad women," he continued. "There are bad men though, just as much as there are wrong men. But there are very few bad women."

Mr. Dunn also said that you should remember that there is always someone who loves you and cares for you as you are, and who will accept you, no holds barred... that someone is God. One cannot expect to have such a perfect relationship with any human being. It would be asking too much. Human beings are naturally selfish and cannot completely sacrifice their pride and ego and give their entire heart and soul to another human bein.

———

It really hurts to admit it, but I think I have figured out the way Monroe thinks of me. He thinks of me very much like my sister Gretel, like the daughter of his friend, like a kid, not like an equal. But he also likes to go to bed with me, and the two are not related. It's different for me, though. The two aspects of our relationship mingle in my mind. It's hard for me to remember that he doesn't feel the way I do. I should try to see things the way they are. But I am too often blinded by my attempts to see things as though they were about to become, at any minute, the way I wish they would be.

Monroe is a friend. But I need somebody to love.

He said that he didn't sleep with my mom yesterday. But who knows.

My mother is so happy. She finally got a job offer. She'll start next month. She said she'd take me to the beach any weekend I want. She's acting so sweet.

My only worriment is that if I ever really get close to my mother, and we talk about sex and everything else, then I'll want to tell her about Monroe. And if I don't, I'll feel dishonest and incomplete and a little guilty, especially if she thinks she knows everything. But there are some things that I just can't talk about. Things that would really hurt her. She'd start thinking of Monroe's and my relationship in relation to herself and she'd be hurt hurt hurt. I don't want to hurt her. And I have to think of Monroe, too. He doesn't want to hurt her either. It's really a pity, because I wish I had someone like her to talk to, not someone gossipy like Kimmie, but someone who cares about me like a mother is supposed to. That's exactly what I need. It's sad and kind of unfair.

———

Dear God in Heaven,

I wish I were older than I am.

Monroe's known so many people and been so many places. I've never been away from home and I don't know anything about anything and I don't understand anything anyway.

I feel so upset. It feels like there are little weights hanging from my heart that swing and tug every time I move, every time the wind blows.

Every photograph I have of him is from the time when he and my mother were in love and living together. Every smile you see him smile has nothing to do with me. There are no pictures of me with him. How could there be?

Why is he so old? Why am I so young? Half the time he expects me to understand everything so he doesn't bother to be sensitive. I feel like I'm caught up in a big wave and I don't know what's happening. I bet you think it's kind of funny, actually. I bet you've been laughing the whole time.

Well, I wish he was seventeen... no, I don't. If he were seventeen, I wouldn't like him. I want him just the way he is. I want everything the way it is. If it doesn't work out, that's just too bad. I'll probably know him for the rest of my life unless he dies.

In twenty years, I'll invite him to tea and have him as a house guest and he can play with my kids and talk with my husband and give me funny secret looks from across the table as we sit over our summer lunch outside in the sunny quiet back yard with weeping willows and wisteria hanging over the porch. There will be a slight breeze and the sound of tinkling wind chimes, and a tear will force its way from my eye when he

In twenty years, I'll invite him to tea and have him as a house guest.

smiles at me tenderly because I'll know he's thinking about how it used to be. I'll have to excuse myself because I'll be crying and my husband will be confused but I'll tell everyone it's all right, I'll be down in a minute..

———

Dear Everyboy in the World,

There was one of you standing in the shadows, leaning against a Chevy in an alley in Chinatown last night. You had your hands in your pockets and your head was tilted to the side and you kept staring at me. Believe me, I would have gone with you if I had not been with Mr. Dunn. I wish you were here now. I wish I had a boy of my own. You had on baggyish light blue pants. You had wavyish brown hair, thick and just a little bit long. You were wearing a white shirt with no buttons or zippers, just a slit to show your chest and to make it easier to get out of.

That man, Mr. Dunn, said that he noticed me on the bus because I was looking all around, and seemed so curious about life, and also because I kept changing seats. I always do that, just to get different viewpoints. I hate sitting in one place for too long. The Chinese girl who was behind me when I first got on was popping her gum so I was chewing gum too to drown out the sound of her chewing and popping, and Mr. Dunn said that I sure was chewing a lot of gum and I seemed to have a lot of energy and spirit.

God, I have to meet some wild guy today. Someone to satisfy this burning... I wish everyone was as horny as I am... I love cute guys, I really do appreciate them. Dear God, thank you for little boys who grow into big ones. I love a man's body, I love a man's face... a masterpiece, and God's most masterful creation... I want someone rough and tough with spirit and energy, someone to run around with and have fun with and fuck anytime I want. In other words, someone who really likes to fuck all the time. It would probably have to be someone young. Monroe can only do it once or twice then he's through for about two hours. Isn't that terrible? I just can't get enough and his deficiencies don't help any.

I want someone to swing me around, someone who laughs a lot and has an apartment and fucks good and hard and loves to dance and get drunk and fuck and whom I could be myself with. He would also have to be bright, and like to go to museums.

Oh God, you know, you can really feel it when they come inside of you.

I know Monroe would miss me if I wasn't around. I know he'd think about me then because he doesn't know anyone else like me. I think of him all the time.

And that hot breath... dreamy.

And when they're just as hard as rocks and they're stabbing you and you could just scream you can hardly breathe it is so 78vghjftgj46z356uzsfyubyuib78cx5742q24xr68v680 b790[79[v689pc568ozx3463455y-w46uc46759v689pvyuiuilv679

I love music. Music makes me so happy I could die.

SUNDAY, AUGUST 1

Little Monroe,

The problem with me is that I find it difficult to separate our little sexual affair from our relationship as friends. I mean, you seem to think of the two as separate entities... like two different relationships with two different people. You always treat me the same way you treat Gretel, and you don't realize that the only natural way for me to feel about you now is very different from the way Gretel feels about you... my feelings are those that would be expected of someone who has been intimate with you.

And I am very confused because you have always told me that you were afraid I was going to become jaded with sex if I kept fucking all those guys I don't really care about, like Ricky and Fred or people I don't even know, like the guys at the party and in the park or that black guy.... Well, as far as I can see and understand, you're doing much of the same thing with Patsy and Karyn and my mom and that wild stewardess of yours. You're always contradicting yourself, and it gets slightly confusing after a while. Oh, Kimmie also belongs in that list with the stewardess.

You are always so busy with your athletic nutritional supplements that I never get to see you. And you can't come back with the argument that you called on Saturday or Sunday, because you said you'd call in the evening and you didn't. What do you expect me to do? Waste my entire night waiting for a measly little call from you so you can ask me to type more labels? Or so you can invite Gretel and me to the movies when you know that I can't stand being with you and Gretel at the same time? It makes me feel that you're trying to tell me that you feel the same about us both and none of our intimacy has ever counted to you. When we're around Gretel or my mother, you treat me like some little twerp. You take advantage of the opportunity to treat me like a stupid kid because you know I can't say anything about it.

Of course, maybe you don't like me very much in the first place. Don't think I haven't considered that. You probably are seriously bothered by my pushiness. Well, I don't really care if you don't like me. It's not my fault that you got involved with me and I'm not going to make any excuses for myself.

It would make sense to assume that you are treating me in such a mediocre way because you're afraid if you drop me cold I might go straight to the authorities and you'd go to jail and everyone would hear about it. I'm not saying that I would do that, but you probably think I'm capable of it. Which goes to show that you don't know me at all if you think I'd be so low-down as that.

Maybe you're bored with our relationship (if you can call it that). Well, I can't argue that it's going anywhere. It makes me depressed sometimes to think that you really don't give a hoot about me and that you're fucking me just because I'm there and I'm only fifteen years old.

Maybe the situation is just as much my fault as yours. Sometimes I think I'm self-destructive. Monroe, I'm just trying to make you see that it means more to me than nothing. In fact, sometimes I just can't stop crying about you. Otherwise, I'm mad at you. I guess I should realize that my reactions are triggered by changes within myself and not by anything you do or don't do... so don't feel as though you've done anything terribly wrong—I'm just trying to figure out how things really are because I really don't understand at all. Maybe it is simpler than I think, but on the other hand, I think you over-simplify things.

I guess you'd better destroy this letter immediately. How sad. It took me so long to write it. My good time, worth $1.50 an hour.

Love, Minnie Goetze Jr.

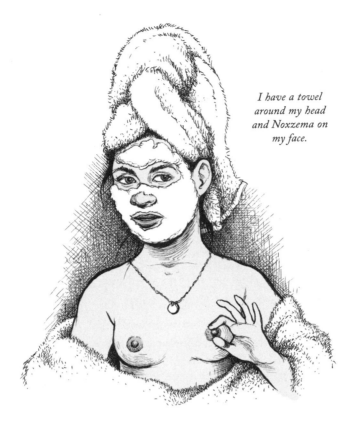

I have a towel around my head and Noxzema on my face.

MONDAY, AUGUST 2

A body can depress you. You wonder: "Is it fat? Is it ugly? What does it look like from behind?"

Here I sit, naked. I have a towel around my head and Noxzema on my face. I think I look better with no clothes on. Clothes break up the body, sometimes making it seem awkward. Some people have good bodies for clothes. Other people were probably meant to roam the countryside naked, living the life of a nomad. I personally feel that I am one of those people. I would be much happier if the burden of worrying about what looks best on me... the burden of going shopping for clothes... the burden of thinking about whether the kind of clothes you wear make you seem like a certain kind of person... if all these burdens were to be removed, I can speculate that I would be a much happier girl.

———

Monroe never even acts like he wants to do anything anymore, if you know what I mean. Like it would be too distracting. He never even kisses me when he leaves, even when no one is around for miles. And he's so irritable. I think he's too involved with his nutritional supplements and it's going to get even more complicated, with new related products, new flavors, magazine and radio ads and famous sports spokespeople, as soon as sales go up.

He just talks to my mother all the time and acts like a damn "grown-up." Nothing I say is funny or interesting to him anymore.

I told him I can't take it. I told him I hated my mother and Gretel and that I hated him, too, and I was going to run away with Kimmie and move to Philadelphia and I never wanted to see him again.

"It's all just as well," he said, "In fact, it's better that way. I've given it some thought, and what with your mother and all... she's beginning to suspect! You make it so obvious, so impossible! I'm only human," he continued, "whether you realize it or not, and I have feelings, and it's hard for me not to get emotionally involved with someone I'm so close to. I can see where this could lead us to falling in love or something." He said this last part with disgust, as if being in love with me would be unpleasant, an inconvenience, at best.

He said that my mother asked him if he was falling in love with me. He denied it. "What am I supposed to tell her?" he said, "that I'm only half in love with you?"

Then she asked him if there was anything physical between us. "Of course not," he insisted. "Are you crazy?"

And my mother seems pissed off at me all the time again. She drinks more when she's mad. Her face is always red; she's always blurry now, and when I tell her, she just gets furious and says, "If you and Gretel would only stop your goddamn fighting!" So I guess it's us that makes her drink. All she does is complain about us.

WEDNESDAY, AUGUST 4

I hate Monroe.

His balls have shrunk. He's civilized. There's no more savage juice left in his groin in his chest or any other erogenous zones. He seems really gay and kind of washed out.

"You don't even look like a man to me anymore. You look like an empty box of Athlete's Nutritional Supplements with a name and address stuck on it."

It's the truth. All he does is work and his head is full of figures and directions. His eyes look glassy and he never looks anyone full in the face. He's always bent over some papers. He goes to bed with pretty stewardesses and he thinks he's leading a full and satisfying life. Maybe he is. But it doesn't seem that things are going to turn out the way he's always told me he hoped they would. He wants a farm in upper New York state that he wouldn't have to live on... he would have other people work it for him. He just wants it to reassure himself that he still is tied to the land in some way. But he'll go on working... I know that he's going to turn out like every other businessman... like the ones at Kaiser he's always condemning.

He just called this instant.

Ring.
—Hello?
Hi.
—Oh, hi.
I seem to have misplaced some really important notes–have you seen them around?
—Wait... they have little X's... on two xeroxed sheets and two stapled-together pieces of handwritten paper, right?
Oh, right–Gosh, thanks, that was notes from a really important interview I had... I'll make you special assistant to the president, $50,000 a year.
—I'm looking forward to it.
I'm taking you out to dinner Friday night.
—What if you're too busy?
No, I'm taking you out. We'll go to that restaurant Rue de Polk. It's French.
—Well, just make sure you remember.
I will, and thanks for finding that paper. You're a good shit.
—You left it on the chair. Fuck you.
Friday night.
—Yeah.
Well, bye!
—Bye.

I'd even go as far as saying that he makes love like a businessman. He didn't even look at me. I was sitting beside him, petting the cat. He just lifted my hand and placed it between his legs. Not a word. His eyes remained glued to the tv set. After a while, it was probably during a commercial, he remembered to kiss me. Then, he turned back to the show as soon as he heard gunshots.

...he turned back to the show
as soon as he heard gunshots.

I didn't really enjoy it. Fucking him satisfied some biological urge, but something was missing, as usual. It just wasn't enough. I had to cry. He never understands why. He hates it when I cry. I cry because I cry. There just isn't anything else to do. It's better than just settling back to the way we were and finishing up the cowboy movie.

He says I shouldn't be so pushy about sex. It turns him off. He says I should be cool and a little more hard to get.

I made two hot-dogs with ketchup and relish and mustard. I didn't enjoy eating them as I imagined I would. They taste different from the kind you get at the circus or at a baseball game.

I've been working hard on Athlete's Nutritional Supplements lately. Two or three hours a day, which is a lot, since I only get paid $1.50 an hour. My job is to type the names and addresses on the labels and put the product in the box. There's a completed order on the table now, ready to be shipped pdq to a Mr. Johnny Bean of Bowling Green, Kentucky. Most of the orders are for just one or two bottles, and Mr. Bean's order is no exception—he's getting a bottle of the amino acid tablets, and one of the super-charged chewable vitamins. *Congratulations on your wise purchase, Mr. Bean!!*

My room is filled to the brim with empty boxes that Monroe is saving for the larger orders. Dirty laundry is draped all over them... labels and stationery cover the floor. My filthy room is his warehouse. My teeth feel funny. The cat jumps around in all that crap and my room really looks like a pigsty. But I don't care. It's always been like that. I don't think there's been more than two months' worth of days in my whole life when my room was clean. I'm just not a very neat person.

This hot-dog is going to make me sick but I keep shoving it into my mouth all the same.

I keep my diary, which is a black loose-leaf binder, under my mattress. I don't think that's a very safe place to hide it. I also have a little *Hello Kitty* diary that I keep in my back-pack but I don't use it that much because I prefer typing. I have a feeling that they will be found eventually. Things like this can find no refuge in an honest home. It doesn't really matter where I hide them. Monroe wants me to burn every trace of anything I ever wrote about him. "Things like that are always found by mothers." So what. I don't care. I'll never destroy it. How else can you remember your life? But she'll probably disown me when she finds out.

I feel very shaky after eating that hot-dog. It was really sickening. Ooooooooooooo. I was drinking some store-brand 7-Up too. I wish I could throw up.

I am so chilly.

I think that Monroe should hurry up and get married if he wants to have kids... he's getting old... he's thirty-five. When his kid is twenty, if he goes at the rate he's going, he might be sixty... If I'm pregnant, I might have it. I'd name the kid Henry. Or Desdemona if it was a girl. Monroe's favorite girl's name is Nicole. I hate that name.

I feel ill ill ill ill

Dear Monroe,

Let me tell you... I know you think I'm fat but I don't care because I know that black guys the world over and also Italian construction workers and wetbacks and old men and also some lesbians like fat girls even if you don't so there.

I hope you are enjoying watching all those beautiful thin girls performing superhuman feats on the TV.

FRIDAY, AUGUST 6

The lights at the top of the Mutual Benefit Life Building just went on. It gets brighter in this room and darker outside the window. All the lights across the bay seem to blink on and off like frantic beacons.

I am in an office on the forty-fifth floor of the Bank of America Building. Monroe is here, too. I came with him—he had to meet Jane Schultz. She's typing some Athletic Nutritional Supplement crap for him. He probably fucks her too and she probably thinks I'm just somebody's harmless kid sister tagging along for the ride.

Carpet-covered partitions divide the room into offices. The radiators are white and streamlined and the tops form windowsills. The carpet is goldenrod yellow, with nary a footprint to mar its plush surface—it has been freshly vacuumed. I guess the janitor was here just before us.

It's very quiet... the fluorescent lights hum and Jane types. I would feel very strange being fucked in this place. I would be scared. We're up too high. And there are so many typewriters here. This doesn't seem like a place where human bodies should move about unprotected. Lust is found in the strangest places, however. I can see getting raped here. I wouldn't be scared because rapes are meant for places like this.

Monroe is wearing gray pinstripes on white. A suit, you know. And a white shirt that is comfortably unbuttoned at the top, with a bit of his hairy chest peeking out. He is tieless, with shiny new penny loafers, not his usual tan suede Earth Shoes or running shoes. I suppose he's trying to look professional, but he's so big and awkward he looks like an ape with fancy clothes on.

I wouldn't put my kid's pictures on my desk if I worked here. Imagine their bright faces smiling into the cold humming atmosphere of the night. It's really horrid. Inhuman. I wonder which demon planted the idea to build this monstrous building in whosoever's head. Oh, it's just terrible. Really unnatural. I feel like I'm made of plastic.

I wonder if Monroe is wondering what I'm writing about. Just more garbage, as usual. He always tells me don't leave my notes around. Someone will find them.

———

Monroe dropped me off at home and then he went back to pick up Jane Schultz and take her out to dinner to reward her for her efforts. Of course I just felt like a little idiot who was in the way. He doesn't appreciate my work at all.

Let him have his stupid, colorless life. I tried to start a conversation in the car. He was rude as usual.

—Monroe.

What.

—What's your favorite color?

Green, like money.

—No, really.

I don't know. Blue. Why the fuck are you asking me such stupid questions?

—Just let me ask you a few more things. What's your father's name?

I can't tell you that. You'd use it against me.

—ok. What's your son's name? I know all about him.

Jesus Christ, come on, lay off it. Let's talk about ADNS *Power Tabs!*

—I don't want to change the subject. Why don't you ever talk about your family? Are you ashamed of them or something?

Just lay off me. We're almost to your place.

—You're such an asshole.

Come on, I really appreciate everything you're doing for the business. I've just got a lot of things on my mind.

—ok, fine. Well, I hope you enjoy your little dinner with Janie.

Oh, don't get bent out of shape. I have to do that. She did me a favor.

—Sure....

I'm baby-sitting for the Golds tonight.

Minnie dear,

I have here a pair of pliers and a crude sort of ballpeen hammer, which I expect is quite old. I sit at the white laminate table in the breakfast nook and type on the old typewriter. An Underwood upright.

It is hot. I had to dig and dig in the big closet but I finally unearthed my old fan. The blades did not turn at first because a dent in the grille covering them inhibited their movement. I've fixed it all up now, though, with my little hammer and my pliers.

The fan blows a cool, gentle breeze directly at my face. The imported air smells of fried eggs—it must have been drawn from the kitchen. The stirred-up air is doing my mind good.

Have a pleasant day, dear.

From yourself.

Kimmie's gone for a week....

Dear Kimmie Minter,

You won't believe what happened last night. I went to a movie with Monroe because he said I needed to expand my mind and we needed to do something besides have sex. So I was resentful as we sat in the theatre, the Alhambra on Polk, seeing a ridiculous movie, "Robin and Marian," because Monroe likes Sean Connery. Towards the middle of the movie I had a strange feeling and I turned around and there was Pascal two rows behind us, staring at us! He did not even smile. After I saw him, he got up and left, without a word! And I can't remember if I did anything that would make him believe that Monroe and I are involved.... I don't know if I leaned on him or touched him so that Pascal could see... I'm sure he followed us there! There's no way he would have gone to see a film like "Robin and Marian" on his own! He would choose something that he could argue had a little more "intellectual meat," although he cried when we all watched "Love Story" on tv a long time ago... his unexpected display of emotion was moving, actually.

I am now on the 3 Jackson bus heading towards Union Square. I am sitting beside my sister Gretel—she is breathing heavily. I told her to cut it the fuck out and she said, "No! Fuck you!" She stopped anyway.

We're going downtown to buy new shoes and maybe some other things. Mom gave us her credit card and a note.

We are now at Macy's. Gretel is trying on a pair of Adidas Vienna sneakers. She always gets dressed up to go anywhere and the strange thing is she almost always wears dresses, never pants. She has a sense of pride about her appearance that I have never had and she bugs the hell out of me.

I think that at least three-quarters of San Franciscan men, excluding Orientals, are homosexual. At least every man worth noticing. Here in downtown San Francisco, every guy I see, yes, *every one*, looks gay. I could croak. I was walking down the street the other day with Chuck and every man we passed gave him the once-over. Maybe it's his beautiful long blond hair or his striking Sgt. Pepper jacket. I know he's going to turn gay eventually. If he can't get it one place, it takes only logic to deduce that he's going to go to the place where he gets it the easiest.

SO MANY GAY MEN.

My knee is touching one right now. He's trying on a pair of loafers. Very preppie. And the worst thing is that most of these men are women-haters. It's very threatening.

I can't wait 'til you return.

A poem:

    A little gizzard slithered out of a wet pile of the same,
    And, gesticulating wildly,
    The blind little clump of irritated red membrane
    Hopped from plate to table.

It cracked wide open and a pixie wriggled out.

Another poem:

> Had a little peanut, a little peanut, a little peanut,
> It cracked wide open and a pixie wriggled out,
> All crumpled and wet unfolding gradually as the sun
>   dried his wings.
> He had a little bag in his hand in which there was contained
> About thirty dried beans and some old razor blades.

TUESDAY, AUGUST 10
11:36 AM

Dear Kimmie,

I am on the 55 Sacramento bus. I have to go downtown to deliver something for Monroe's business. Then I'm having lunch with my stepfather, Pascal MacCorkill, at a French place called Le Central. It's a really expensive restaurant and Pascal eats lunch there all the time with his authors. He called my mother yesterday and said he saw me at that movie theatre with Monroe. But my mother already knew we were going to the movies, so she didn't think anything, except that Pascal was trying to do something evil by poisoning her brain.

The guy I was supposed to give the box to wasn't in. I therefore left the box with his gorgeous blonde secretary.

Now I'm in the restaurant. They know Pascal by name. Here he is now. I saw him through the window. He has a big smile on his face.

LATER

Pascal said today that I shouldn't hang out with Monroe, that men don't normally take young girls to movies unless they have an ulterior motive. I laughed. He asked if Monroe ever did anything like make a pass at me and I said, "Not everyone has a dirty mind like you, Pascal."

As it turns out, Pascal is moving to New York in a few weeks. Suddenly and out of the blue he was offered a job at a very prestigious publishing company and he'll be pretty high up, in charge of some division. I was surprised and felt kind of sad. Even though I hardly ever see him, I still knew he was around.

THURSDAY, AUGUST 12

Monroe is in the other room watching tv and chatting with my mother, Charlotte. I feel confused and disoriented. Monroe seems perfectly happy, lighthearted, laughing with Charlotte, but when I was alone with him in the living room for a moment earlier he radiated hostile resentful irritated emanations. He asked me where my friends were and why don't I go find them and said he wanted to spend some time with my mother.

It is not a lit-up streetlight hazy darkness like most nights; it is a black crisp night and my eyes are like headlights. I feel like I've wandered into someone else's life and don't remember where I belong. It is depressing to think that Monroe is tired and bored with me and that he won't tell me so because he doesn't want me to get upset, because if I get upset, I might tell my mother. It makes me feel quite anxious to imagine what he's thinking. I think I shall get drunk. Yes, I'll go take a hot bath perhaps with a snucken beer beside me and then I'll drink the hidden sherry... no, that seems pointless. Where would it get me? Especially if Monroe leaves while I'm taking

The left side of my room.

a bath or something typical like that. He'd leave without saying goodbye to me and I'd feel even sorrier for myself. Then I'd get frustrated and I'd cry.

It's 3:00 am. I made a lot of money tonight sitting for the Golds. They paid me more than they owed me because it was such a long night. I fell asleep on their bed watching tv. They went to some huge gala event at the Civic Center. It's Friday the thirteenth and the party had a "funky occult" theme. Mrs. Gold was all in slinky black, with glittering gold eye shadow and nail polish.

I like Mrs. Gold. She speaks French with me. I love speaking French. I've had it a few years at school, and I pay no attention to grammar, but someone gave me a few volumes of *TinTin* in French and they really helped me learn. Mrs. Gold says I've got a good accent.

Mr. Gold was in a very good mood, and told me who they saw at the event. Herb Caen, the columnist, and Mayor Moscone, and Armistead Maupin, the gay writer who's writing a serialized novel for the *Chronicle*. And a few actors. Mork from Ork, and some of the cast of *Beach Blanket Babylon* (some of them are friends of Mrs. Gold). And Boz Scaggs, who lives right in this neighborhood.

And Mrs. Gold is very happy because she got a role in a paper towel commercial. She plays a lady cop. She's going to say something like "These cheap paper towels are a crime."

Dear Diary,

Perhaps today marks the end of an era of my life. I don't think I will be seeing Monroe much anymore. He is going away again tomorrow and won't be back for two weeks. He's going to make important contacts for his company in big East Coast cities.

By the time he gets back, I'm sure he will have found other people and more efficient ways to handle the Athlete's Nutritional Supplement business. He won't need my help anymore. I told him he should hurry up and get married if he wants to live to see his children grow up. At the rate he's going, he'll probably be at least forty before he has any.

And in September, I'll be going to a new school all the way across town on Ocean Avenue.

Mom will have started her new job, at a women's club library on Union Square.

And Pascal will be gone.

I finished another comic. "Identity Crisis."

I'm not sure if I like it. It seems so crowded. Maybe I'll try to draw larger frames or something... but I really like drawing small probably because I'm near-sighted and I see better close up.

Chuck came over and I showed it to him. He's the only one who's seen it—he doesn't draw, so I wasn't worried that he would judge it harshly.

"It's really cool! You should do a whole book!" He said he'd lend me his collection of Fabulous Furry Freak Brothers. I'm not really into drug comix. The Freak Brothers are three wacky pot-smoking hippies and they've got a greedy, mangy cat with a raccoon tail.

Chuck pulled out two fifty-dollar bills and waved them in my face.

"Lysergic Acid Diethylamide," he says. "LSD."

Yeah? Like, so what, Chuck? Are you asking me to put two and two together? Are you bragging about your success as a drug dealer?

One of his older brother's friends makes the lsd in his garage. He's a straight-looking guy, he's an accountant, has a decent car, and lives in a nice little ranch home in Burlingame.

Chuck's been selling the acid at concerts, and on Polk Street and Haight Street, and to certain people he knows from Urban.

He asked me if I would consider letting him keep a vial in our freezer. He said he'd pay me to do it, no problem. He's worried that his brother's wife might find it if he keeps it at their place. He's not ready to get kicked out of there until he passes his ged.

I said go ahead, you can put it in the freezer. He said I can take some whenever I want it. It's a little clear bottle, looks like eyedrops.

I spilled a bottle of ink on my bed and I didn't notice at first that it had spilled and the ink had time to soak all the way through 2 blankets and a sheet. I didn't notice it until I felt something wet on my butt—now I have a huge black stain on the back of my jeans.

My second comic: Chuck came over and I showed it to him.

I got a postcard today from Ricky Wasserman. He's in Europe. I kept turning it over and upside-down looking for clues but there weren't any. There was a picture of a castle on the front of the card, and in a tight, childish but controlled hand on the back, in letters so tiny I almost needed a magnifying glass, it read:

Mme.

Europe is more beautiful than I ever could imagine. First we arrived in Iceland. It is always daytime in the summer. The midnight sun is a cool orange blue filling the air with a wonderful eeriness. Then Luxembourg. Enchanting cathedrals and cobblestone walks. Then Amsterdam. A gorgeous city, canals, bridges, and prostitutes. Then a bike tour through Holland. Beautiful countryside. (Totally level.) Dutch people are definitely what I would call the beauteous race. Tall, blond, and skinny. (You would love the men as I love the women.) Today is my first day in Germany. Lovely so far. Tomorrow we ride out of Heidelberg taking the "romantic road" along the Nekar River amongst ancient castles reaching for the sun. (How poetic) Then the Black Forest; home of "Grimm's fairy tales." Then if time and muscles permit we ride the "Rhine River" then S. France. Then home to the sunny surf.

Now that we're thousands of miles apart I think of how we never got close to each other. I had some really wonderful times with you. And I think of you a lot. Maybe we went about it wrong. I was in a jerky mixed phase. (Romantic but real) I hope to see you again and spend time with you. If you're really moving to "Philly," then I wish you best of luck and best of love. You're one of a kind and I love you for it. This letter must end before it twists itself into a rut.

Love, Rick

I feel sad.

I've been talking less and less. People have begun to comment on my silence. I think more, I suppose, and I'm less nervous. I was looking back at some things I wrote a couple of months ago, and it occurred to me that I sounded very bitchy. I wonder what people will think of me if they ever

The right side of my room.

read this. I don't really care. Sometimes they accuse me of being cruel and irrational. I don't often think of what other people think of me. Kimmie says I contradict myself constantly and that I don't think before I say things. It gets her flustered sometimes. When my mother's mad she tells me I'm irresponsible like my father. Her friend Burt thinks I'm hateful and manipulative. Pascal thinks my vocabulary is deteriorating. He is disappointed in me. Monroe thinks I'm pushy and childish, at least I think he does. I wonder if he knows how much I love him. Someone said that I was secretly a sensitive person but that I hide my truly affectionate feelings.

My mother asked me when I'll be finished typing, so I guess I'll stop. Goodnight, sweet dreams, Love, Minnie.

SATURDAY, AUGUST 21

and from this wretched body I speak
Saying it will be different when I die
When I cross the Nile to the west
Wading knee-deep in thick muddy waters
Entangled with roots of the papyrus
That lace the shores
I will depart this heaving pulsating vessel
It has a soul of its own
There it will lie, to be consumed
By the earth. By some raven or hippopotamus.

When I die I would like to die by
Drownation in the Ganges River
I want to wade in knee-deep, my sari billowing
    up around my thighs
My toes curling around the sucking mud fouled
    with the charred
Remains of Indian priests
Lap lap lap the water so vast along the shores
    so many miles apart
The hum and twitter of foreign voices
    unaware of my separation
From them

...I would like to die by drownation in the Ganges River...

Scum floats on the water almost stagnant
   it flows undetectably
Slow and deep to the ocean,
    towards skiffs and outriggers
    and barges and canoes and plankton
    and whales and sharks

My heart beats wildly my eyes fight the closing lids
A fly settles on the water
I do not take a breath I sink, the water consuming me
I suck in the muddy black poison
The last taste
My brain is bathed in the black stench
My heart fights and is freed in a muted scream
All my love encased in bubbles that rush to the surface
And burst

WEDNESDAY, AUGUST 25

Two letters from Pascal arrived today, but he sent them a few days apart. He hasn't left for New York yet, but I haven't seen him since we had dinner a couple weeks ago.

Dear Little Minnie:

San Francisco is shrouded in fog. I cannot see the bridge from my kitchen window. It's cold. Horns are mourning away under the bridge, out somewhere beyond the Golden Gateway. There won't be many sailboats scudding around the bay in this greengray fog.

Closer to my window—it is early morning—there is the little garden. Red fuschia cascade down through the ivy; white daisies, elegant and pristine, dominate the spaces between the evergreens (daisies seem to flourish in San Francisco). Here and there a lonely red rose languishes sad and propped up by the faggot gardeners who tend the little garden. There is last of all an exquisitely delicate foxglove, light blue and healthy, brazenly healthy, against the wall.

The summer, I am beginning to notice, is nearly over. In two weeks I will have been transplanted to the Big Apple. It saddens me that I have had so little contact with the people I love this summer. Soon it will be autumn and then what?

I brought you here with high hopes four years ago. I am leaving you here with some regret, and with the hope that you will realize that there will always be a special place in my heart for you.

Love, Pascal

Dear Little Minnie (not so little):

The foghorns are mournfully depressing this August morning. Can you hear them too? I'm going to sail this Sunday. It will be the first time for me on a sailboat on the Bay. Maybe the last for a long time. One of our editors, John P—, owns the craft.

What a pleasure to receive your card. I too would rather talk to you, see you, than write.

I'll have some vacation time after I settle in New York. Maybe I'll go to Tahiti and wear a sarong, go native as they say. Sit in the sun and contemplate my navel. I might even take up meditation. So think of me when you hear the mournful bellows of the foghorns. 'Cause I'll be elsewhere, as they say.

Our little nuclear family seems to have fallen apart. All very depressing of course. Maybe it will have a happy ending.

The summer will be over soon. Again, you'll be starting a new school. A new chance to prove yourself academically, as I know you are able. A clean slate, so to speak. You will make lots of new friends, interesting friends. And there will be new challenges.

I am fine. I've found an apartment in Manhattan, big enough for you to come visit. I'll expect you.

Work will keep me very busy.

I'll miss you.

Love, Pascal

THURSDAY, AUGUST 26

Kimmie was going to come over this weekend but called today and told me that she decided to go to Paradise instead, with her mother and father. I don't see how she can dare show her face there again, after seducing her cousin's husband. I'm glad she's not coming here. It's a relief. She doesn't interest me. She rejects intellectual stimulation. I feel like a bitch saying that, but it's the truth. I outgrew Kimmie a while ago, and she's becoming a hindrance.

TUESDAY, AUGUST 31

Dearly Beloved Diary,

Today is the day after Monroe returned from the East Coast. Words are not able to describe the warm euphoria that fills my body with every fresh San Franciscan breath I take. Why, just the day before yesterday, I was hardly aware of the beauty around me.

I could barely contain my joy when Monroe stepped off the plane.

He's taking my mother out for dinner tonight, but he said tomorrow it would be my turn—we have to talk business. I guess he still wants me to work for him! I'm so happy, I want to send my mother roses!

THURSDAY, SEPTEMBER 2

Pascal has moved to New York. My mother has started her new job on Union Square at a private library. My sister is at her friend's house. She stayed overnight there last night. I'm too tired to clean my room. I just want to go to sleep.

My Junior Year

I wallow in a state of despair,
but by and by,
I am befriended by a girl
named Tabatha.

———•———

I have to take a bus and BART.

Today was my first day at Lick-Wilmerding, my new school. It's a less expensive private school and sort of a technical school. They have metal shop and wood shop classes and a football team. It used to be a boys' school, but it's been co-ed for about ten years. It's bigger than Urban, a lot bigger, and I can't walk to it. It's a sprawling collection of rectangular white blocks with blue trim, way out in some non-descript mostly residential middle-class Chinese/Spanish/white neighborhood, next to the freeway. I have to take a bus and bart. They are taking me on a probationary basis because I did so badly at the other schools and they only accepted me because they thought I was good at art.

It is so stupid, so boring. Among the students here there are only a few token smarties. At all my old schools, everyone was smart.

I hate my mother. She always says the wrong things. For instance, "I don't see how you can complain about this school. You could have stayed at boarding school! You could have stayed at Urban!" It's the truth, too. I've ruined practically my whole life as it stands now. I should have stayed at boarding school. Urban was my redeeming chance, but I screwed that up, too. Now I have to make do with going to that fucking Chicano school all the way across town.

I'm crying... can you believe it? I just can't help feeling sorry for myself. I feel like I'm drowning in a sea of banality. I only know uninteresting people. How can I say that? I'm probably just as boring myself.

Sometimes I want to kill myself.

Monroe is just about completely ignoring me. He's taking my mother out for drinks tonight. My head is swimming in a poison serum; something is attacking my brain. I feel so horrible.

FRIDAY, SEPTEMBER 10

It always ends up the same way. He kisses me and all wrongs are supposedly righted.

When will it ever end? There's nothing passionate, nothing explosive, it's like a steady busy signal, and I become more frustrated the longer I have to listen to it. But it would be hard to end... he's been a part of my life for so long, so very familiar that if he left I would never be quite the same. I've known him since I was twelve, since we moved to San Francisco.

He asked me if I wrote in my diary about going with Kimmie to the beach and all that... I said it's not his business.

"Look," he said, "if you want to keep a diary, fine. It's probably a good thing for you. But how 'bout you keep it at my place?"

I said no way because I bet he'd destroy it and then lie and tell me he lost it. Then he wanted to know where I hide it and I wouldn't tell him, but I'm going to start moving it around

———

The classes I'm taking at school are:
French 2 (3 units)
English (Utopian Literature) (3 units)
Geometry (3 units)
Mechanical drawing (2 units)
PE (1 unit)
Chemistry (3 units)

SATURDAY, SEPTEMBER 11

Monroe said I'm depressing to be around. He said he was bored because I'm a teenager, and that he can understand my enthusiasm about certain things because he was once a teenager too, but nevertheless, it bores him.

The first time we made love, we still had on our jackets and our shirts. And he still had his socks on.

I still don't know if he believed I was a virgin or not. I had never even kissed anyone. He said, "I can't believe you're a virgin." I don't know if he was kidding I hope he was kidding please tell me he was kidding otherwise it meant nothing and it was all just lost and there is no love there's nothing

When he wasn't in the room I looked in his jacket and found his wallet. I wanted to see if he made one of those cards that Earl Nightingale says you should have when you make your 30-day test. I was hoping I could learn something about him, something deeper than what he's shown me. He did

He did have a card.

have a card and what it said was that he wants to start his own business and make a million before the age of forty. That's all he wants. And I already knew it because he's talked about it. He doesn't want anything of the spirit.

Why am I crying? I want to tell him that I love him, but what good will it do? He seems so completely self-interested. I feel so lonely. Boys my own age bore me. I just can't get really interested in them. I don't want to play games.

I wish I could move to India.

I wish I could live on a farm with R. Crumb and Aline. I wish that they were my good friends. I could go live with them and watch them work and learn stuff and do chores to help out. I think they're happy. I wish I knew someone who was happy.

Dear Monroe,

I'm sorry I'm so miserable. I know it turns you off, but I just can't live this way. I can't not live this way either. I miss you so much sometimes. I think I love you. I really try to hide it—maybe I'm afraid of rejection—but now that I've been rejected I suppose I can tell you. My life, my energy, is all directed in the wrong ways. My youth is something that cannot be helped. Every minute I spent thinking of you was futile.

FRIDAY, SEPTEMBER 17

Last night I asked Monroe if he was busy all weekend. I wanted to know if he wanted to make love. He replied that he was not only busy but also sick and couldn't find enough time to do everything he had to do as it was.

I got so mad and full of hate and bitterness that I threw my typewriter across the room. I just didn't know what else to do. I cried, but there just wasn't any way, it seemed, to appease my anguish. So I went to bed with the intent of visiting him the next morning before school. I wanted to yell at him and hit him and tell everybody what he's done. But I didn't feel like it in the morning and I went through the day with hate pouring out of me—even into my work—I couldn't even draw—I couldn't control the lines, they sprawled wildly all over the page.

I sat in the library and wrote a letter expressing my feelings, I cut math, and took the cable car to his house. I rang the buzzer and left the note in his box, thinking he wouldn't be home, but he opened the door with a mechanical button from his apartment so I held my breath and went in. My heart was beating so fast.

He had been taking a nap. I told him how miserable I was, but tried not to appear too miserable.

"Yes, yes," he said. "I understand. It makes me feel shitty to see you so miserable." He was being kind of funny. He told me I looked like a ragamuffin, but I didn't care because I knew I did and I wouldn't care anyway.

After a while he said that he guessed it would be a big mistake for us to make love because it always affected me so much.

"I either have to love you or hate you," I said. "I just can't be casually in-between like you seem to be with your relationships."

We talked and he kept pulling my hair and tugging my arm. Then he put his arm around me. I protested a little, but then I let him, I don't know why. Then we took a nap. I got up after a while because I hate sleeping in the afternoon. I walked behind the bed, over near the table, and he suddenly sprang up and grabbed me. "I simply can't have you searching through my things!" he said.

"I know!" I cried. "I wasn't searching. I was just getting some fresh air. I can't sleep during the day."

"Come take a nap!" he said.

I didn't come so he grabbed me and pulled me on the bed and put his big legs around me. I couldn't really get up, I just squirmed. I knew he could feel my waist and my butt and my tits kept rubbing against him, but what could I do? I didn't want to be in that position. Finally, I relaxed. I was laying across his chest so we formed an X. He kept rubbing his hands over my back and under my shirt and over my ass, and said, "Look now, you're getting me excited, you have such a good body...."

Then I asked him if we were just going to keep doing that. He said, "If we made love, would it screw you up?"

I said, "No. I won't be jealous I won't be sad I won't get involved."

We were trying to decide whether we should or we shouldn't, then he moved my hand down between his legs. He was already hard. I rubbed his chest then we took our clothes off and I sucked his cock and then I fucked him and then he fucked me the phone rang twice and we finally came and then we kind of went to sleep. He was rubbing my back it felt so warm and naked we hardly said anything after that. We had already done it and we probably shouldn't have.

He said if I could hold on and keep it together, that we'll be able to date when I'm eighteen. We could go to the movies together without being paranoid. We could take a trip on his sailboat. For sure he'll have a sailboat by then.

I stole $2.75 when he was in the bathroom.

SUNDAY, SEPTEMBER 19

A long time ago, I was sitting in Bob's Grill on Polk Street, and a girl outside at the bus stop blew a kiss at me. I remember her very clearly and I'm almost certain I saw her last night.

I went to the *Rocky Horror Picture Show* with Chuck and Kimmie at The Strand, a shabby theatre on Market Street. It's a pretty stupid movie about an innocent couple who get mixed up with a group of alien transvestite sex fiends. Nevertheless, it was fun because there were so many people who seemed to know the whole thing by heart. They were singing all the songs, and lighting up matches or lighters at certain parts, like when the song said, "There's a light... over at the Frankenstein place..." The whole theatre glowed.

It was really really fun. We got high and played Fascination in a big arcade before we went in. It's a game where you drop a quarter onto or

*There were so many people
outside the theatre*

beside piles of hundreds of other quarters on a glass shelf in a glass box.
There's a pusher arm that pushes the piles and the point is to make your
quarter be the one that causes the pusher arm to push the piles of quarters
off the shelf, in which case, you win them.

Kimmie bought two sheets of acid from Chuck because she thinks she
can sell it in South City.

There were so many people outside the theatre waiting for the midnight show—lots of gay guys in Frederick's of Hollywood and high heels.
Such beauty I have never seen! I was so happy. Chuck knew a few of them
because he sells acid around there... I'm telling you, I think Chuck must
be bi because he seems pretty at-ease in that environment. But of course
he says he's not.

I met Richie, an incredibly beautiful guy about nineteen, with wavy
brown hair and dark eyes. He's tall and thin and paper-white and he was
practically naked, in a black corset and sheer black stockings and 6-inch
platforms, and lipstick and mascara on his sweet face. He was in line in
front of us and he was so nice to me and he wanted to braid my hair and
I let him. He was so gentle, and his voice was like a warm "coo" in my ear.

The girl from the bus stop was in line way ahead of us. Richie said her
name was Tabatha and she's a bad-news baby dyke.

I said, what do you mean, "bad news"?

And he looked at me with his finger on his chin and laughed and said, "Oh, forget it, honey!"

He said she hangs out on Polk Street, and that's where I saw her.

MONDAY, SEPTEMBER 20

Dear Diary,

I do not have to go to school today because I am sick. You won't tell—I always fake.

The sun shone through my open windows this morning, drenching the garbage, the debris, and the salvageable filth buried beneath it with a brilliant glow.

I hopped from my bed at 8:33 am. I had been dreaming, wading down the center of a creek going uphill towards the summit of the mountain, the trees about us growing more and more profuse. Monroe and I were naked, hand in hand, salmon slipping between our legs.

I hopped up and washed my face, brushed my teeth, and inserted my contact lenses. *Je me suis maquillé* and then I pulled on a pair of red tights and squirmed into a pink on pink dress of my mother's, then her pink leather Capezio sandals and a purple silk Mao jacket. I gave myself a lovely crown of braids that I would never wear outside.

Here I sit, dressed as such, cat basking at my feet in the morning sun.

10:02: Now the pretending becomes a hindrance. I mustn't do anything too lively; that would be cause for suspicion. I must take my flashy clothes off and slip into my nightie or I will be blamed for having "too much spirit to be sick." I can't play my records loud and I can't ride my bike.

WEDNESDAY, SEPTEMBER 22

Monroe is on the wagon. He's taking dilantin and antabuse and my mother made fun of him, calling him a teetotalling churchlady. He said whatever, his doctor said he had to cut down. If he drinks when he's on those pills, it will make him throw up and turn red and break out in hives. And if he tried to stop drinking without taking the pills, the doctor said he might have convulsions.

He says he just has to settle down a bit and not have too many upsets or distractions because he's doing a second weekend of est training and he wants to be really sober, not just stop drinking the night before.

Here I sit,
dressed as such.

Mother's friend Andrea came over and Mom made a delicious tofu dish but I didn't eat it. Both Gretel and I hate tofu but my mother always makes it.

Andrea has such long red hair.

After dinner they were in the living room and I asked if I could play my Doors record. They said sure. They were smoking pot and when "Crystal Ship" came on I heard them moaning and squealing and when it was over they called me and asked me to play it again. Right now, they are lying on their backs, with cushions under their heads, with the lights low, smoking a joint. For the last half-hour I've been entertaining them by putting the needle back to their favorite song after it ends so they can hear it again and again.

> *Before you slip into un-con-scious-ness*
> *I'd like to have another kiss,*
> *A-no-ther flashing chance at bliss,*
> *Another kiss, another kiss.*

They are still in the other room, laughing. I'd better to go tell them I'm going to sleep.

...they are lying on their backs, with cushions under their heads ...

My adventures alone, without love, without things to eat.

I woke up this morning and decided not to eat all day. My mother and I ran all the way down Lake Street on the new bike bath, very early, when it was still dark and foggy and quiet.

I am sad.

When Monroe came to our house after his est seminar he acted as if he barely recognized me, and what could I say? I felt weak, my eyes would not lift, and I could not laugh. "At least I am not eating," I thought.

Later, towards nighttime, in the back seat of our little lime-green Super Beetle, I felt unsteady and definitely not in the swing of things. Mom and Monroe sat in front. "It's all Greek to me," my heart sighed, as I sunk back and turned away from their full-grown evening talk... I'd heard about it all before on the evening news....

"Patty Hearst sentenced...Presidential campaign... Legionnaire's disease... Werner Erhardt... brainwashing.... "

I understand, yet I am not really involved. "Time will pass quickly...," I thought, "why do I love him?" And, "To eat nothing, nothing, nothing, isn't it exciting? Oh, if only this could be a permanent thing."

"Tuesday," he said after my mother parked and trotted into Cala Food Market to buy their gallon bottle of Almaden white Chablis and her Benson and Hedges Menthol 100s and my Abba Zabba bar if they have any, Bit O' Honey if not. There we were, alone for a moment. "Tuesday, we will go to the movies. Or Wednesday."

"OK," I said, "I guess so." I am thinking now that I would also like dinner. Yes, dinner and the movies. I will be hungry by then, and yes, dinner would be wonderful.

Will we make love then?

I am so bored at school. I hate it there. I want to be in Egypt. I wish I were high in the Swiss Alps tending a herd of goats. I wish I were stoned. I wish I were in his arms I wish I were in his bed.

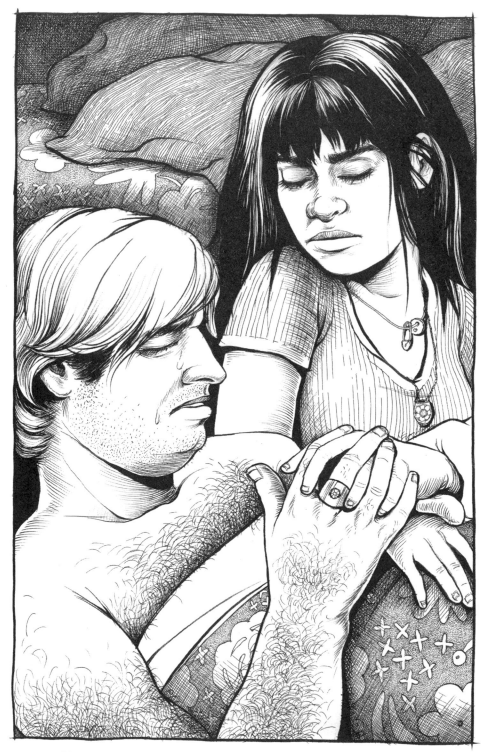

Monroe had a bad trip and became increasingly uncomfortable and started to cry.

SATURDAY, OCTOBER 2

I took some of Chuck's acid with Monroe last night at Monroe's apartment. Before we took it, he was bragging about how he used to drop acid in college every weekend.

I thought it was weak acid because I didn't feel anything but after a while I saw colors on the wall, moving, like projected wallpaper, but it wasn't particularly interesting or fun.

However, Monroe had a bad trip and became increasingly uncomfortable and started to cry. At first I thought he was joking. I never saw him cry before. He was afraid to be on the bed because that was level with the windows, and that made him nervous. He made me lie down with him on some pillows and blankets on the floor. He didn't want me to leave, even to go to the bathroom, and he kept asking me if I loved him, didn't I love him, do I still? So I told him I love him over and over, but it was never enough. And he cried and cried and said he loves me he loves me he loves me, again and again.

He was afraid and weak and he needed me but I felt distant and confused, a kind of detached excitement, a perverse pleasure, because I'd finally found what I'd been looking for but now I had no desire for it.

SUNDAY, OCTOBER 3

When I saw Monroe today he said he had a bad trip and that he didn't remember anything. "Don't even tell me what I said or did, I don't want to think about it." Fuck him.

LATER

Kimmie called. We're going to meet Chuck down on Polk Street.

Essay Question:
Read the end of Book Four closely—the part from the
time Gulliver leaves the Houyhnhnms until the conclusion.
Examine Gulliver's attitudes carefully.

What do you think were Swift's intentions by having
Gulliver react the way he does? What is his satirical point?
Remember that Swift is not Gulliver.

Fuck it.

And then, he goes on to say, "What dirty old man like me wouldn't give anything to be fucking a fifteen-year-old regularly?" And then he says (while I was crying), "Let's drive around the corner for a minute."

We stopped in some shaded area a couple of blocks away, and he asked me to suck him off. I asked him to fuck me and he said, "I thought you'd be satisfied with giving me a blow-job." I kept sobbing and he kept repeating that he knew how I felt, he knew how painful it was, for he'd been in love once himself. If he was, then why couldn't he understand that I didn't want to just get his fucking rocks off? He stroked my hair and guided my head down towards his lap and I sucked him off, choking and sobbing all the while. I wanted to make love, but after he came he just zipped it back up and we drove back home and he was all pissed because I was still crying.

Everything is so loveless and mediocre.

Maybe I'm just a loser when it comes to love. I love people, but I can't show it, so they never love me. I am so sad.

I think I'm going insane.

I think I want to run away.

I feel like Monroe is such a bastard, but then, I can never tell for sure—sometimes I think I'm dreaming. He tells me I'm overreacting and I get confused and I don't know whether I'm overreacting or not. I don't know exactly what I'm thinking or how I feel or what to do next. I feel like really beating the shit out of someone.

Maybe I can meet a girl like Tabatha.

Everything is so loveless and mediocre.

Oh, boy I'm tired and feeling overwrought. How would I become underwrought? If I stare into the sun, with my lips parted not eating not sleeping speaking not a word?

Tomorrow will be another day.

I don't think Monroe would kiss me if he had just come in my mouth. I always try to avoid a situation where the question would arise.

I hate men. I hate their sexuality unless they are gay or asexual or somehow different from the men I've known. I hate men but I fuck them hard hard hard and thoughtlessly because I hate them so much. At least when they're fucking me, they're not looking at me. At least I can close my eyes and just hate them. It's so difficult to explain.

Goodnight.

THURSDAY, OCTOBER 7

Dear Joe,

I am filing this report on ward #6789, Minnie Goetze.

She is restless, sporadically inattentive, and does not feel like doing her homework.

She is lonely, and wishes someone would make manifest any love they might have for her by hugging her. She is not sure that anyone does love her, and I am not sure, either, although I haven't looked into it to much extent.

And why doesn't Monroe love her, not even a little bit, not even unnoticeably, like he'd love a sister or a daughter? Does he really not love her? Doesn't he know that she only wants to hug him and kiss him and sleep with their bodies together, not even sexily, just together? She would love to cook for him (and she really can cook—but why doesn't she ever want to cook in front of him? It's almost as though she's afraid to show her grown-up side to him). But she loves him and would like to be with him and show him the things she really likes, and she wants to read to him and have him listen. She wants to sit on the beach and kiss his little blonde head, because she really does love him.

I'll keep an eye on her.

Let's don't let Minnie go insane, not yet at least.

Thanks a lot, Joe.

Love,
Mickey.

FRIDAY, OCTOBER 8

Dear Joe,

It's me again. This time, no report on #6789.

I'll remain in close contact.

SUNDAY, OCTOBER 10

I saw Tabatha at *Rocky Horror* and she shared a joint with me. She said, "I see you everywhere, girl!" She's got a tough, feminine style. She sat with me through the cartoon, before the movie. It's always the same cartoon, the Betty Boop with the song "St. James Infirmary Blues," sung by Cab Calloway.

While she sat next to me I tried to look at her out of the corner of my eye while she watched the movie. She is so beautiful that her beauty seems like an impossibility. I want to describe her but I'm afraid I'll ruin it for you. Her skin is so smooth, and poreless, and seems to glow from within. Her mouth is large and so expressive when she sucks on a joint it looks like love. She's just one day older than I am but she lives nowhere, and everywhere, goes to no school but knows everything. I don't even want to talk about her eyes when they flash in my mind I get dizzy I just want to consume her I want to be her.

I tried to look at her out of the corner of my eye.

Tabatha left as soon as the Betty Boop was over. She had to go find the people she came with. She kissed me on the cheek, and I could feel her warm breath in my ear when she said she really wanted to see me again, like, we should do something....

TUESDAY, OCTOBER 12

I'm in the school library.

I have several complaints, as follows:

I hate the location of this school. By the freeway in a depressing neighborhood.

I hate Roger and John and lots of other people.

I let John fuck me in the bushes behind the hockey field because:

Because he got me stoned and I don't know why I felt like if I didn't he would hate me, he would think I was leading him on because I got stoned with him it sounds so stupid writing this, writing makes it clear that I bring horror upon myself because I am an idiot

I don't want to go to school ever again

I know he'll tell everyone

He's so ugly and stupid

I hate myself I hate him

I don't ever want to see him again

WEDNESDAY, OCTOBER 13

I just cannot do any more math. At one point for each problem that takes me ten minutes to do, I simply can no longer see any gain in finishing the assignment. It would be easier to choose problems at random to study for the test.

School is so draining. I come home physically and mentally tired and bored, sick and anxiety-ridden. School ruins my whole day. It leaves me in a catatonically depressed state. I usually cut a few classes and come home early. I just can't stand it, you see. It's boring, boring, boring.

My body is getting to be in terrible shape. I sit down too much and get stiff and tired and my feet fall asleep and my back hurts. So I've been trying to get more exercise. Tomorrow I go to school and deteriorate just a little bit more.

THURSDAY, OCTOBER 14

My mother talked to the principal at school and he said they had to put me on academic probation because I cut too many times. They said they want me to go to a therapist as a condition of the probation.

My mother was crying in the car and saying that I was so, so lucky that they didn't kick me out because now there's no other school that would take me.

FRIDAY, OCTOBER 15

Monroe left for New York again.

SATURDAY, OCTOBER 16

I slept really late. I feel weird from that angel dust. I wish I hadn't smoked it. I wanted to talk to Tabatha but I was way too stonedd

———

I am going out to dinner tonight with Robert, the guy from Cosmo. I'm going to meet him at Miz Brown's Feed Bag on California and Laurel because I don't want him to see where I live. Good-bye.

LATER

Robert seemed to really like me over the phone, and I guess I liked him, we had such long conversations, but half the time I was pretending to be someone I wasn't, and it was easy because he couldn't see me. Sometimes I was just slightly different, the Minnie I wish I was, more confident. Less sad. Prettier. But when I met him, I realized that he was exactly the same as I thought he would be, he never pretended, he was honest.

We ate on Geary at some Thai place with little rooms with woodwork everywhere, and pits you dangle your feet into when you sit on the floor. I just couldn't talk to him. It's like I just couldn't set my face right. I couldn't rearrange my features or change my expressions to match the person I felt I should be. I didn't know who I was, I didn't know what he wanted.

He's twenty-four, already finished college and has a job. He thinks I'm seventeen, almost eighteen. I got served wine. He speaks slowly and thinks about what he says, he's not sarcastic, he stared at me a lot and I was afraid that he was thinking that I'm not as pretty as he thought I'd be. He's pale and soft-looking, with light brown hair, sort of bland really, but with brown eyes that were beautiful and stared at me seeming to ask questions but I just wasn't anybody, I couldn't be anybody. I tried to bounce him back with my eyes but he was looking too deeply.

After dinner we drove to Ocean Beach. He wanted to take a walk along the beach in the dark, but we didn't because it was raining. I've been there at night before. When the weather is clear, people light bonfires up and down the beach and have parties.

We parked on The Great Highway overlooking the ocean and watched the rain fall all around us. It was sort of embarrassing to be there because there were lots of other couples parked there too. It's a real make-out spot.

We sat and talked a little and he pushed a tape into his 8-track, the volume down low.

Knights in white satin, never reaching the end....

He kissed me so I kissed him back.

No one could see into the car because of the heavy rain.

I let him fuck me in the front seat but still all the while I had this feeling that he thought we should stop and that it was going too far, but that *I* was supposed to be the one stopping it but I didn't want to talk to him anymore I just couldn't. I just wanted to get everything over with and go home. I started crying afterwards. I tried not to but I couldn't help it.

He drove me back to Miz Brown's and I walked home in the rain. He said it was silly that I wouldn't let him just take me home. "You can trust that I am who I say," he said, and he showed me his driver's license. He asked me if I would go out with him tomorrow and I said yes I didn't know what else to say.

SUNDAY, OCTOBER 17

I just ate three large theater-size boxes of candy. Why? Because the movie scared me. *Burnt Offerings.* And Robert was holding my hand. I didn't know how to make him let go without him grabbing it again. I didn't want to be touched. And Robert smelled like the same after-shave he wore last night. I just wanted to leave and the movie scared me.

I took a lot of Ex-Lax so maybe I won't feel like I ate all that candy.

I've been obsessed, I think, with cooking and being orderly with my little notebook. It's been getting me nervous and quiet. I have to plan all these meals and shop and cook. I've hardly said anything to anyone all week. It makes me feel like I've been sleeping in the sun and I just woke up—do you know the feeling?

I think women are beautiful. Tabatha is beautiful.

But then I was scared just now and I was with someone who was practically a stranger. I've only slept with him once I think I was very drunk. I don't want to get drunk or stoned and I don't want to get fucked anymore. I tried to tell Robert that I couldn't see him any more. I said I'm just really busy with school so I couldn't really make any plans right now. He seemed a little pissed.

I wish Monroe would never come back. I don't want to think about him or any other man touching me again. I don't know why I let Robert fuck me. I'm never going to see him again.

I don't like men looking at me when I walk down the street. I don't want to look at their eyes.

I keep thinking about Tabatha. I can imagine kissing her and it feels so much purer and sweeter than kissing any man.

TUESDAY, OCTOBER 19

Such a mean letter from Robert:

"Dear" Minnie,

You are a very attractive young woman. I knew you would be even before I first set eyes on you. Now that I know you, I can say that yes, you are attractive physically, but your personality just doesn't measure up.

I have never met anyone so negative about everything. I get the feeling that you don't feel any joy in your life. When I'm sad or mad, I can look at the smallest flower or the face of an innocent child and suddenly feel happiness. I don't think you could. I feel sorry for you.

You are so cold. I can't believe that I ever "made love" with you. If you didn't want to be with me, why didn't you say so? You hurt me.

When I look into your eyes I see emptiness. It scares me.

I'm glad that you are out of my life.

Good Luck to You Always.

Robert

———

I went to a psychiatrist today. Dr. Alfred Wollenberg. He used to see Pascal and Mom when I was at Castilleja. He asked me if I minded. I said I don't care as long as he never talks to them again. He's a very, very old man, with a dark, cluttered little office at 450 Sutter, downtown.

"First things first," he said. "Let's first address why you're doing poorly at school."

I'm supposed to go to see him once a week. I told him about Monroe. He promised he would not tell my mother, but the reason he gave is that it would not help me.

A letter from Pascal:

Dear Minnie,

I don't know why you cannot organize yourself to buy a 15-cent stamp. There is a dollar enclosed just in case you're broke.

What's new? Are you even thinking about which college you'll set your sights on? Never too soon to start thinking about that. God, it has been a struggle. Now Gretel is on the skids. You know, I have concluded that forcing middle-class kids' noses into the trough of education is ridiculous. What is the point of it? Tell me. If someone is curious he/she will respond and seek enlightenment. If not, then it is just painful—and expensive.

Do Starsky and Hutch talk about their interests in music, theatre, the arts, literature, science, mathematics, evolution, sociobiology, economics, history of ideas, or gourmet cooking? Christ no. They are men of action fighting the pestilence of crime. And they do look cute—but have you ever seen how real cops look? The necklace—gold chain—tight jeans, Adidas running shoes, products that can be bought that make one "look" like Starsky. Even s and h dolls.

Did you know that I always had an interest in "art"? I just bought a LeWitt silkscreen. You'll see it; you might like it. And I did buy a triptych (3 prints) by Arakawa. Then I bought a couple of lithographs by an "unknown." He is a teacher of lithography at Pratt. Earlier I purchased two eighteenth-century prints of "turkeys"—these from Florence. So don't think I'm not interested in your art, for I am.

However, you don't need my advice on education. If you do then "seek and ye shall find."

Like most people, I suppose, I am enslaved by my own experience. When I was growing up—poor and surrounded by enormous ignorance—I needed advice. I got none. Now I have a head crammed with good stuff and my children—biological and "adopted and raised"—don't give a shit. Now there is human social evolution at work.

The reason I work in international publishing is to offer my ideas and experience to education—in the service of education. What I'd give to have one child who was "turned on" to similar interests. You and I can at least communicate with honesty. Maybe you'll use that talent of yours to inform all of us.

Just remember that I love you even though you are neglectful.

Pascal.

A letter to myself.

Dear Minnie,

You really are the greatest. I love your cooking; those diet chicken enchiladas and the bran muffins especially. You make pretty all right toast too.

And you draw real well. I don't have to tell you that. My goodness! You just finished another one-page comic! Good for you! I think you're really smart and clever, even if those around you do not. I think they're jerks anyhow. Real creeps. Who needs 'em? Screw 'em, I say.

I forgot to tell you. R. Crumb came over to your house with his band to visit your mother because they were playing in the city again and wanted to practice somewhere for a few hours, and without your knowing it, he sneaked a look at your sketchbook. Do you remember how you were copying some of his drawings so you could learn how he shades with pen and ink? Well, he saw your practicing and look what he did!

Well, he saw your practicing, and look what he did!

And I really have to hand it to you for taking the initiative and teaching yourself how to cook. And you're really learning, not just about cooking, about everything, let me tell you. At least you're beginning to see where you want to be and what you want and how you're going to get it, and you're building a set of morals while you're at it. Those assholes don't seem to know in which direction they're heading.

But you, you chose a simple life as your goal. You want to find a good man, settle down, have kids, cook, draw, and paint or die trying. And maybe even do comics. You want to love someone, love your life and stretch your talents to the fullest. That's admirable.

You're doing pretty well. You're trying not to drink or get stoned anymore. And you've got legitimate, personal reasons. It was your free choice. And now you have chosen for yourself an unpromiscuous sex life where the one you love and the one who loves you is the only one who's going to get what you got to give. You learned that from experience. It hurt a lot, but that pain set you in the right direction away from it. I wish you strength.

You have things to look forward to. You're not just floating. Tomorrow, you'll ride your bike and learn how to make shrimp fried rice and baked apples. Next week you hope to have lost two more pounds, and you'll be starting your own illustrated cookbook. Next year, it'll be time to start looking for a college. Life's good and you love it. It's pretty, like a picture.

> Good-night,
> Love,
> Your Fairy-Godmother

THURSDAY, OCTOBER 28

I had a little scare today.

This afternoon, I went jogging in the neighborhood and when I got to Arguello Street, I suddenly remembered that I had left my diary on my bed!

I ran back. I was totally out of breath. Mom was talking on the phone in the kitchen. My diary was still on my bed. I stuck it between my bureau and the wall and got a band-aid from the bathroom. I told Mom I had a blister. Then I ran out and jogged for about a half an hour longer.

My third comic: It's got Jesus in it.

SATURDAY, OCTOBER 30

Last night I went to Monroe's apartment.

I decided to walk there because I didn't see anyone I knew on Polk Street. He asked me if I wanted a beer and we both had one. We talked for a while. He asked me if I missed making love and he said he did too. I was a little bit scared before we made love and while we were, I kept asking myself, "Why? Why am I doing this?" It's been more than a month since the last time—I always knew we would again, but I imagined that it would be me who suggested it, and I thought there was a chance that he might reject me.

Yes, but he reached out to me, and made me realize that he had missed me. "We never talk anymore," he said. He was so affectionate, and I watched him, and I talked to him, but I was confused, and only thought, and didn't feel, and didn't know how I wanted him or how he wanted me.

He seemed so lonely. He talks so quietly sometimes. I think I want to love him, but I don't know if I can trust him. Is a relationship between us two so impossible? I'm almost sixteen. I feel more like a woman every day. I just don't want to see him lonely. I don't ever want him to feel like I have felt.

It's strange. I take it for granted that he will be a part of my future. Sometimes I am sure that we will get married someday. I don't actually think it, or feel it, it just seems inevitable. Because I just can't imagine living without him.

One part of me knows he's an asshole and a jerk and I'd be better off if he were dead. But the other part of me doesn't believe that and is sure that one day we will all live happily ever after, one way or another....

He always said that maybe when I turn eighteen, we might be able to have a real relationship. Now I'm almost sixteen, but I'm so tired of everything... I don't see how I could have any feelings left in two years. It seems so far away.

MONDAY, NOVEMBER 1

Last night was Hallowe'en. Me & Kimmie got very stoned and walked all the way to Polk Street. I had to beg and bribe Kimmie to walk because she was wearing platforms. I love walking, especially on a beautiful, clear, and amusing night like last night. We weren't dressed up—we just went to

We saw Richie at Buzzby's with his boyfriend.

look. The street was packed. Just men, men, men, in all sorts of costumes: Dorothy, Frankenfurter, Magenta, Village People, and of course lots of guys in leather chaps with their bare asses hanging out.

All the discos were wide open, and mirrored disco balls were spinning and reflecting all over the street. The music was very loud, solid disco.... We squeezed in and out of Buzzby's and Kimo's and The White Swallow. I always wanted to go into those places but we always got carded before. But last night it was so crowded that no one noticed. We saw Richie at Buzzby's with his boyfriend, who is at least thirty and very macho.... Richie was in a blonde wig and we hardly recognized him at first... he's so much in love... it was so loud you could not hear anything anyone said.... Kimmie and I were screaming at each other at the top of our lungs.

I feel looooooooooooove.

We were walking past that alley where people get blow-jobs and it always smells like pee... there's that chi-chi coffee store on the corner—and a man in diapers and a mask ran out into the crowd with a chainsaw going full force! We were really scared, we thought he was going to kill someone. But it turned out that the chainsaw didn't have a blade or a chain, whatever it is, in it.

As usual, I was hoping I'd see Tabatha but I didn't.

WEDNESDAY, NOVEMBER 3

I told Dr. Wollenberg that I think I want Monroe out of my life. He said he didn't think I'd have much luck because of the dynamics between my mother and Monroe.

Wollenberg gave me a brand new orange vibrator! I've never had such a thing. He had a pile of boxes behind his desk. He bent down to grab one, and at first I thought he was giving me a shoebox. "Why would he give me a pair of shoes?" I thought. An immediate but fleeting image of pink Mary Janes came to mind. I was prepared for embarrassment. But I opened the box and there was a full-color pamphlet with a picture of a woman rubbing a vibrator on her cheek... inside, a young man rubbed a different model on his cheek. "Relax...," it said. "Make time for yourself with a Sunbeam Personal Massager."

He said if I really wanted to separate from Monroe, the vibrator might make it a little bit easier, as a substitute for sex. He asked me if I ever had an orgasm, but I wouldn't tell him.

"Well, you'll be able to when you learn to use this vibrator," he said.

I was embarrassed, but I took it. I'm afraid to use it though because it makes a lot of noise. If my mother or Gretel sees it, I can tell them it's for my cheeks.

Dr. Wollenberg is a very old man, probably nearly seventy. It occurred to me that he might be a pervert, but as he makes his ideas clear, it seems more likely that he is not. His office is in a building downtown near the Stockton Tunnel. It's tiny and the upholstery is dark red and he keeps the Venetian blinds closed.

WEDNESDAY, NOVEMBER 10

What is it like for a mother and a daughter to be secretly jealous of each other over the same man? Does my mother *really* not know about Monroe and me? Does she really believe that Monroe is just a kind, platonic companion to her daughter, taking me out to dinner as a public service?

I was sitting in the living room with Monroe. We thought my mother was asleep. The phone rang. I ran out to the kitchen to answer it. There was my mother—she had been sitting in the dark in the breakfast nook spying on us. She fumbled and backed away, pretending that she had just woken up.

I converged with Kimmie and Chuck at Nito Burrito on Polk Street at around five o'clock. We sat in a booth next to a window and drank coffee. They were telling me how Tabatha is such a sleaze... they heard that she's got real problems because she was in porn movies when she was a kid. They said she's a junkie and she cheats people. I argued with them, but they know I have a crush on Tabatha and that love is blind and I should listen to them and just stay away from her.

Just then who should rap on the window?

Just then who should rap on the window, right next to my head? Tabatha.

She came in and asked if I wanted to go shopping with her. I said sure. We left Chuck and Kimmie there. Tabatha said she doesn't dig them too much.

She turned me on to a Quaalude and we went down to Market and got our pictures taken in one of those booths at Woolworth's. We each kept two pictures. We both looked so high. I felt really good on that Quaalude. You feel happy and your body feels like it's floating....

We went across the street to Kaplan's, an army surplus store. I sat on the floor near the dressing room while Tabatha stole some pants. All she did was try the new ones on, then put her old ones back on the rack. They never notice, she says. As long as you put something back.

That's how she shops.

Tabatha wanted me to go to *Rocky Horror* with her tomorrow but Elizabeth's coming.

Elizabeth only stayed one night. She flew back home to Los Angeles this morning. Castilleja has a mid-semester break for everyone but the juniors, who have three days of pre-college test prep.

Pascal met Elizabeth in New York a few weeks ago when she was in the East to look at colleges. She met him at his new place. She said the apartment building is beautiful, near Central Park, with a doorman and polished brass and marble in the lobby. Very Eloise. He took her to a pretentious French restaurant for dinner.

Should I be jealous? He is obsessed with waspy-looking girls with small tits. Like Elizabeth. He thinks David Hamilton is a great photographer. I don't think he would actually try to fuck Elizabeth but Monroe sure wanted to the time she was really drunk and threw up in his car.

Elizabeth says Pascal writes postcards to her when he travels to interesting places.

She's applying for early admission to Sarah Lawrence.

Last night we bought some alcohol at Manwell's liquor store on Sacramento Street near my house. Manwell never cards anyone. He's a quiet middle-aged Arab man with a potbelly. My mom even sends me there to buy wine for her. Elizabeth suggested Hereford's Cows. They look and taste like milkshakes but they've got a lot of alcohol mixed in... there are several flavors. We chose banana and mocha.

We took a walk and ended up at Alta Plaza. We sat on a wall and drank the Cows. Because they taste so good, you don't realize how drunk you're getting. We got very very drunk. Elizabeth got all teary and too scared to walk home. She said she's not used to big cities. We caught a cab on California Street and she cried the whole way home. She was too embarrassed to go inside the apartment because she thought my mother would be angry because she was drunk. As soon as the cab stopped to let us off, she jumped out screaming, "You hate me, you hate me!" She took off down the street sobbing. She gets this way when she's drunk, crying, threatening to kill herself, and she doesn't remember anything the next day. I didn't go after her, I was sick of it, so I went inside but Elizabeth never came in. My mother called the police because she felt responsible and she was afraid Elizabeth might commit suicide, and the police came and used their spotlights on the front of our building and down the block and they found her around the corner about half an hour later.

My mother was pissed but she let us go shopping downtown this morning. We hardly had any money so we just walked around and talked. We stopped at a little store to get some soda and candy and we saw that they sold chalk. We bought a box, then found a good spot in front of one of the windows at Brooks Brothers and drew pictures on the ground of Santa and reindeer and a big bell with a ribbon. We wrote, "Happy Holidays!" People were staring at us and we started singing Christmas carols, even though it's not even Thanksgiving yet. People gave us money as if it were the most natural thing in the world. They smiled. We made about $16.00 in an hour, and we were pretty excited. It was incredible that Elizabeth had overcome her shyness, which is extreme.

Mom picked us up at 3:00 by the Chinatown gate and we took Elizabeth to the airport.

Elizabeth and I started singing Christmas carols.

Letter from Pascal:

Dear Minnie:

You are going to be sixteen in a week or two. That is another mile-stone. Sweet sixteen. On the doorstep of womanhood, of life. If memory serves me right, I met you when you were just four. So twelve years it is. I've known you almost as long as I've known anyone. And, of course, we've shared a few Christmases! I'm happy that I know you. If I were corny or sentimental I'd say that you were one of my oldest friends.

I value very highly any and all communication with you. I only wish there were more of it.

I'm sure you know that you always have a home in my domicile wherever it may be. No matter what, you are always welcome. In fact, that hardly expresses what I mean. You are forever entitled to share whatever I have in the way of room and board. As long as I am at it I may as well say that for better or worse you are my "daughter." Just consider yourself one of those poor pioneer children captured by an Apache tribe, led by another renegade—a mad Scot.

New York is in its Winter Season. The town is full of life: art, music, theater, books and literature. San Francisco is nice, I'll admit, but it isn't for me anymore—unless retirement. It has recently snowed—on me and trees and buildings. Now it's gone.

Soon you will be receiving Human Nature. It will entertain your nimble mind. Some of the future articles—on the light side—are quite interesting. For example: "The Crush." Get it? Who hasn't had a crush? I'm sending Gretel that magazine for teens: Seventeen.

Should I mention school? No. Already I have said all there is to say. But don't waste that pretty mind of yours. It is one of the best and needs developing.

I had dinner with your pal Elizabeth when she was touring the colleges. She tells me she's working like crazy at Castilleja. I hope she makes out all right. She has her sights set on Sarah Lawrence. Very tough and competitive. I can't wait to see where you end up.

"I LOVE YOU." -Pascal

WEDNESDAY, NOVEMBER 17

I will be at the psychiatrist in about an hour. I'm going to tell him that I just can't use the vibrator he gave me last week because it's so sad and too intense it almost hurts. I prefer to be physical with *people* and the vibrator leaves me cold.

I think Kimmie's going to go to the *Rocky Horror Picture Show* with me next weekend. The last time I went I fell asleep during the show, though—I was speeding the night before and didn't get much sleep.

SATURDAY, NOVEMBER 20

First she thought that men were hateful and disgusting and she walked with her head bent to avoid meeting their eyes. Withered penises wiggling loosely in their pants, leering eyes and skinny legs.... But then she'd fuck them and not look at them and not really want them but for a moment, then she'd hate them even more afterwards and never want to see them, and sometimes she cried because she felt so lost and confused and full of hate.

And she got drunk more and more because she felt funny and drinking made her forget.

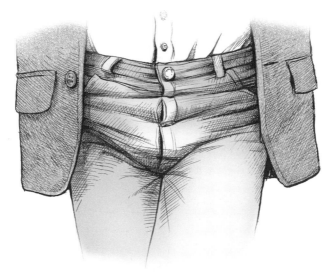

...wiggling loosely in their pants...

One night, she and Kimmie were drunk and ate Chinese food and then went to Broadway, to see if any guys would think they were whores. They went to a porno shop and looked at porno magazines and then they watched an ugly movie in a little smelly booth and picked up two young men from the suburbs who thought they were prostitutes. The girls let the young men buy them drinks in Chinatown and then they went with them to their van and fucked them.

Somehow everything got confused and mean and the guys didn't believe the girls weren't prostitutes and said, "Who the hell are you trying to kid—we know you're whores. *Whores, whores!!*"

The girls wouldn't even take any money but as they drove off, the young men threw a handful of change at them.

Minnie did not feel anything. She didn't even cry. She didn't care anymore whether anyone loved her or not. She realized that she was alone and she didn't care anymore. She just felt hate. And then she knew that she was becoming really screwed up.

She went to Monroe and she tried to explain without telling him anything in particular, and while she explained she cried, and she was so glad she cried because then she felt more like herself and not so numb. And he held her in his arms and she could feel his heart beat and she knew he was the only man she ever loved, with her father and her grandfather and her English teacher from eighth grade, too.

LATER

I just took two of Mom's Valiums to see if they make me feel better. She calls Valium "vitamin V."

> *Car Dieu a tant aimé le monde*
> *Qu'il a donné son Fils unique,*
> *Afin que quiconque croit en lui*
> *Ne périsse point,*
> *Mais qu'il ait la vie éternelle.*

> For God so loved the world
> That he gave his only begotten son
> So that whosoever believeth in Him
> Shall not perish, but have everlasting life.

SUNDAY, NOVEMBER 21

I used to imagine us hugging each other and being warm in his bed and resting my head on his chest and hearing his heart beat. But it just never happened that way. We just fucked and fucked and it broke my heart and now I feel sick.

LATER

I'm going to meet Kimmie on Polk Street. She feels creepy and depressed about what we did too, and we've promised each other to never do anything like it again. I'm not going to tell Dr. Wollenberg.

Kimmie has some speed.

TUESDAY, NOVEMBER 23

Tabatha's birthday is Saturday. I feel like I love her.

A beautiful name....

THURSDAY, NOVEMBER 25
THANKSGIVING

We went to Andrea's for Thanksgiving. We made pumpkin pies to take there. It was depressing. Mom was drinking a lot of wine in the afternoon, and yelling at us because we were fighting over whose turn it was to clean the litter box.

At about 4:00, we decided we were going to walk to Andrea's house with the pies instead of driving. She lives on Baker Street. Mom took a gin and tonic with her in a plastic cup, and we all set off for Thanksgiving dinner, Gretel and I each holding a pie.

About halfway, Mom decided she didn't want her drink anymore so she dumped it, half-full, cup and all, into a mailbox. With letters in it.

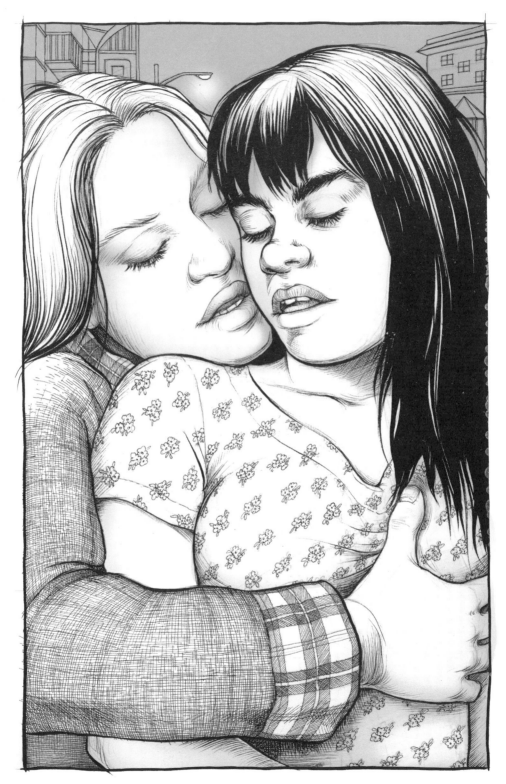

Tabatha embraced me.

I was shocked. I would never do that. What if there was a letter from a grandmother to her grandchild? Or from a little girl, a letter with heart stickers on it, in which she apologizes to her best friend? I think it's against the law, anyway, to tamper with the U.S. mail.

The dinner was even more depressing. Monroe was there, but he was all antsy and said he had to leave early to watch a game with his buddies at the Washington Square Bar and Grill.

FRIDAY, NOVEMBER 26

It's twelve minutes after two in the morning. I guess that means it's really Saturday. At about ten-thirty I went down to Polk Street on the bus—Mom was out at the movies and I just wanted to get out of the apartment. It's weird to be wandering around on the street alone at night so I walked quickly and went into Sukkers' Likkers and bought candy and a ball-point pen. Then I went across to The Bagel and had coffee and drew a little in my notebook. I looked up and I saw Tabatha whiz by so I left and walked down Polk as if I hadn't seen her and there she was on the corner near California under the streetlight talking to some fag.

When she looked at me I suddenly felt all hot and tingly and embarrassed and shy.... "Hi, Tabatha."

"Hey, Minnie! What are you doing here? Where's Kimmie? Don't tell me you're all alone! Take a walk with me?"

We left her friend and she took me to this old school building on Sutter Street, a four-story brick public school, and we went up the fire escape to the roof-top. It was a warmish night, cooling down with the fog, and we kissed and felt each others' bodies but I wouldn't smoke any pot I just wanted to look at her with clear eyes she's so beautiful I almost can't look it's like my mind rejects the possibility of such perfection.

God I just wanted to fuck her but what does that mean with a girl? Would she show me what to do? Would she think I'm an idiot? I can still feel her hands on my tits and her lips on my lips everyone everyone says she's so bad but it's so stupid what the hell could she do to me?

I feel dizzy and I can't sleep.

SATURDAY, NOVEMBER 27
TABATHA'S BIRTHDAY

I feel sad, like there's no purity left.

Monroe took me with him to look for cars today. He said he needed my expert advice.

First, we got some huge sandwiches on Geary because he eats like a fucking pig.

Then I said I wanted to go to his apartment before we look at cars and he said, *"Is that all you think about?* Maybe we can go after. If there's time."

I said I want to go before. He got mad and he said ok but it's got to be really quick. I was pouting and he drove his beat-up little beige bug angrily to his apartment and when we got there, he just wanted me to suck his dick and he came really quickly but I really wanted to fuck and I started to cry. Then he starts yelling at me then he hugs me then we left but I felt terrible.

He says it's for my own good. He thinks I won't get so emotionally involved if I just suck his dick and we don't fuck.

We walked all up and down Van Ness looking at cars in showrooms. He just wanted to look at Honda Civics because, he said, they were new and they were the best. I said they're fucking ugly.

"They're all fucking ugly! *You have such shitty taste!"*

Every place we went I hated the cars. I hate cars anyway. Then in front of one place I was pulling on his arm and he turned around and suddenly punched me in the stomach, right on the street.

SUNDAY, NOVEMBER 28
MY BIRTHDAY

Now I'm sixteen.

They had a little party for me. My mother was there, and Monroe, and Gretel, and Kimmie and Andrea.

They got me a beautiful pink cake and they bought the new Ringo Starr album with that embarrassing song about being sixteen and having lips like strawberry wine.

Monroe was so well-behaved and not sarcastic, not at all, treating me reverently, as though my birthday was a holy rite of passage. He pulled me aside at one point and apologized for punching me in the stomach.

SUNDAY, DECEMBER 5

Tabatha isn't around.

I saw Richie on Polk and he told me that she was arrested for possession a couple days ago and they sent her to some high-security group home in the Valley but no one knows how long she'll be there.

He said he's glad because he told me not to hang with her. He doesn't tell me exactly why, as if he doesn't want to gossip. I know they're friends. He acts like he likes Tabatha when she's around.

Chuck doesn't live with his brother anymore, but he didn't get emancipated yet so he has to live in a group home in the City. He hates it because there's an early curfew. I still see him on Polk Street a lot. He still claims that he's not gay or bi. Maybe he's telling the truth... he still has long hair, and most guys I know chop it all off as soon as they come out.

SUNDAY, DECEMBER 12

Something bad happened to me... almost.

It rained while we were watching the *Rocky Horror Picture Show*. The rain had stopped by the time the movie was over, and it was wet and dark and cold on Market Street at 1:30 in the morning, or almost 2:00, with a few buses on their last run. Kimmie was going to a party in South City but I didn't want to go so I decided to walk home.

I'm so tired. I feel hung-over too, with flashing lights behind my eyes and a stomachache. I was taking swigs off of someone's peppermint schnapps and then maybe I had a joint with angel dust or paraquat or something.

My mother is vacuuming furiously in the hall, knocking the vacuum aggressively against my door.

I always walk on the street, not on the sidewalk, on the street side of the parked cars, so that no one can jump out at me from a building.

I walked from The Strand, up Market to Larkin. When I got to Clay, I took a right instead of a left because I suddenly decided to drop in on Monroe, even though it was 2:00 in the morning. So on I walked, up toward Russian Hill, where he lives on Green and Taylor.

"Get in the car, bitch!"

The streets were empty and wet and the streetlights made bright reflections everywhere, on the streets and on the wet cars. I heard a car coming up the hill behind me with that wet sound like bacon in a frying pan, but I didn't turn around to look. I thought it was just going to pass me but it stopped right beside me and the front door opened quickly and blocked my way forward. I turned my head and a man suddenly grabbed me by the arm and was trying to pull me in the car, right over his lap. He said, "Get in the car, bitch!" I looked down at his hand on my arm, at his bony long black fingers. I saw a shiny bluish gun on the seat beside him but it hardly registered. Somehow my free hand got hold of a bus stop or parking sign pole which luckily I could reach because I was sort of in between two parked cars. The pole was cold and wet and too big for me to close my fingers around it but somehow I determined not to let go, and I felt my fingers lock for me so I could look around, for help I guess, but my voice was frozen. I thought about screaming but my throat wouldn't open.

A couple of times the car slipped back an inch or two because I guess the man lifted his foot off the brake pedal, on purpose or not, I can't know but I thought my arm might rip off.

The man said let go you stupid bitch I'll fucking kill you bitch if you don't let go. He was pulling so hard I felt like I might already be dead but I didn't let go of that pole. My cold hand had become an iron claw welded to the steel post, and suddenly then a cab drove by on the cross street at the top of the hill and he actually saw us or heard us. His brakes squealed as he turned down Clay; he was going the wrong way or else the other man was. The black man saw what was coming. He said fuck. He was maybe thirty-five and gnarled. He let me go but pushed me hard, and I almost fell down as he slammed the door and drove off.

The cab driver got his license plate number. I was stunned but he put me in his cab, let me sit in the front seat. He was youngish and Italianate and breathlessly excited. He had saved me, it was clear, but I didn't know what to say, I was *too* stunned. He drove me to the police station on Vallejo near the Broadway tunnel. The cab driver told the policemen the situation as he had come upon it and they asked me all kinds of questions and filed a report. They made me roll up my sleeves and they took pictures of my arm where the man was gripping me. There were black bruises the size of quarters all up and down my arm where his black bony fingers dug in. The strange thing was when they asked me to pull up my sleeve... I didn't expect anything to be there. I felt kind of like when you're waiting for your temperature to be read and you hope you at least have a small fever or else your sickness might not be believed. But there was plenty of proof all over my arm and they took several pictures.

They told me the man probably would have killed me and the taxi driver saved my life and I shouldn't be walking around at night like that. I said I know I was really lucky about the cab driver and I said thank you.

Two police officers sat me down at a table and asked me if I was drunk or if I had been drinking and I said no, I just had a small sip. They asked me where I was coming from and where I was going to and I said coming from *Rocky Horror* going to a friend's house.

They said a lot of those *Rocky Horror* kids get in trouble.

They let me make a call for someone to pick me up. I said my mother wasn't home so I had to call someone else, her friend, so I called Monroe.

Somehow Monroe was angry when he picked me up, cursing a lot and telling me how stupid I was to be running around at night. He didn't appreciate being called from a police station at 2:30 in the morning—why the fuck couldn't I have called my mother? I think he was actually nervous because the cops might wonder who he was and why he was picking me up. I started to cry and he pulled the car over somewhere in Pacific Heights on Jackson or something and he said Jeezus he just didn't want to have to worry about me and feel responsible for me it's just too much. He cares about me and doesn't want to see me die at the hands of some jerk, but to be pulled out of bed in the middle of the night it's just too much. I was trying not to cry more. I was hugging myself tight and not looking at him but he grabbed me and I said he was hurting my fucking arm then he patted me on the head and said come on now, and kissed my cheek sort of and I sort of looked at him and he said, come on now again. Don't cry. He lectured me for ten more blocks, and then we were home. He went upstairs with me and woke my mother up and was suddenly all serious and angry again, and told her all about the event, and gave her police numbers for the report, and she was pissed. Her face was all shiny and swollen from being asleep and from the night cream she uses. She had on a long white gown and white cotton gloves so her hand cream wouldn't come off.

She wanted Monroe to sleep there. She told me to go to bed. I think he slept on the couch.

———

Gretel is upset because she heard Mom berating me about what happened last night. We were in the kitchen. Mom was scolding me about drinking or smoking pot or something....

Gretel was angry and called me a stupid pot-head and began to cry because she said I'd probably end up dead.

"You're such a disgusting retard! How can I respect you? I hate your guts!" She ran into her room and slammed her door.

MONDAY, DECEMBER 13

The police called and said that the car that black guy tried to pull me into was stolen. It was last registered in Florida. So probably, they'll never catch the man unless he does something else in the same car.

LATER

A letter from Pascal:

Athenaeum Hotel

116 Piccadilly

London

Dear Minnie:

Your letter must have gone astray: up until I left for London town there was no sign of it. The possibility that it will appear like a star on a soft cushion is not forgone. There we are: off to a confusing start.

Well, how are you? Still getting to know yourself? San Francisco. Next it is the world. That might stop you in your tracks. How about thinking of starting off with college? Once you're there, you'd see a lot of other human beings in sort of the same state you find yourself. Not that you'd find anyone like you exactly—you are unique—but other seventeen and eighteen-year-olds "finding out" alongside you. You aren't alone. Dream about it. You may grow to like the idea.

Anyway, you are well loved—should I enumerate?

The next question is: whom do you find interesting? Everyone? Or maybe the question should be: What do you find interesting.

There is always art. And I don't mean doodling or cartooning or whiling away your time escaping the job at hand. I mean lithography, painting, collage, sculpture, etching, potting and other messy but productive disciplines.

There's business. Jeez, ah shit ah wanna get rich and then I'll be a big shot (Gretel's term). I mean, when bereft of imagery you can always make money. "But no; that ain't for you."

Study literature. Hmmm. French, German, Russian (your mother's first love) or Polish—not much there—or Italian—at least Dante, or just plain English. Start with *Pride and Prejudice*. Whatever; don't forget to write it all down.

Why do I care about you? Well, why do I care about myself or Gretel or your mother? I mean, it's just natural, no strain. What can I do for you besides offer you a place in my lush quarters? It is nice to have someone as important as you to care about.

So what are you doing? As I sit here in this boring hotel waiting to go to Cairo then Florence then London then home, I think about how much you'd enjoy taking in the sights. Somehow you seem far away.

Have you seen Elizabeth? She's a smart, funny girl, like you.

There you are. Another communiqué from Pascal. Love. Say hello to Gretel and Mom. And so on. And on and on... Pascal..

———

I guess I'd better start paying attention to school. I think I cut about twice a week. Sometimes I don't go at all, and sometimes I leave in the middle of the day. I try to space it out evenly so my absence isn't too obvious.

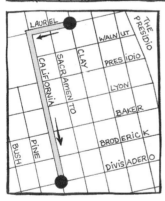

GOIN' IN?

YEAH THANKS

TUESDAY, DECEMBER 14

Dear, Dear Wounded Diary,

My mom searched through my things and found my diary.

She called Monroe.

They called me.

They were drunk when I met them at a bar.

They planned for me to marry Monroe.

Some primitive node in my brain began to pulse with joy.

"Oh yes, my love, he loves me, he wants to take care of me, even my momma wants what's best for me now at the end of this long painful road I shall finally have my warm happiness, the pink glowing love that I needed so badly! Never shall I need again!"

Then something snapped and I was overwhelmed with sickness.

Life just melts into blood and flows between my grasping fingers. I can't save anyone else and I can't save myself....

Every man for himself!

Sauve qui peut!

———

I have seen many ugly things in my life. Somehow the effect is never sufficient. I will always return to the scene of the crime that I have not committed, because I feel responsible.

Should I be ashamed to admit that human deterioration is an eternal source of fascination to me?

Squalor is cozy to me and I love to place myself in situations of potential danger. My recklessness does not please me. I know that my sordid tastes are the expression of a death wish—I want to punish myself—I want to punish other people—I long to be alone but I long to be loved. The pain I feel is leading me into darkness.

WEDNESDAY, DECEMBER 15

Dr. Wollenberg wasn't surprised at Mom's reaction when she found out about me and Monroe. She called him. She was hysterical, and blamed him for not telling her.

He says it makes perfect sense that she wanted Monroe to marry me because she believes that then, all responsibility for what has happened would be taken off her shoulders.

Monroe and I fucked but it doesn't count with me. I stayed overnight at his house and my mother didn't even care. I think she wanted me to. It's like she thinks I'm so fucked up, it's got to be Monroe's fault, so he should suffer the consequences.

It made me feel kind of sick, like I was in some play but it had become real.

I couldn't go to school. I was too depressed.

The men all go to the bar and have a beer after work.

I really wish I were just stoned.

SATURDAY, DECEMBER 18

I am full of worried, nervous, frightened energy. I just don't know.

Sometimes I wish I was big and bold. I wish I could dance like a spook and I wish I had the guts to wear clothes that made me look like a living violin. I wish I could walk like a prostitute. I wish I could kiss the girls and make them want me because I was so tough. I wish I could go up to the girls and grab their titties and put my hands down their panties and make them giggle or scream.

Tabatha's back now. She said she wasn't in a group home, but was in LA visiting some friends.

Those loud-talking chicks really put my heart into fourth gear, let me tell you.

Tabatha is pure in a way. She has never had a pimple and is slim whereas her sisters are fat and greasy.

It's cool it's cool.

Beer and speed and grass and downers, is it really an ugly and sad way to be?

Lovely, lovely colorful daytime. How could you exchange it for a drunken night?

TUESDAY, DECEMBER 21

Hello.

I am at Lambo's and I don't know where I'm going to go. Tabatha just left me here. She went off with some guy. I don't think she told me if she was coming back. I'm not going home. There's nothing there. Nothing.

I'm at Lambo's ... Lambo's... Lambo is a real person. I would have thought it was the name of some made-up clown. They sell hot-dogs here and I see a cotton candy machine but it's not doing anything. There are a few old men drinking coffee and looking out the window. I'm in the corner always I like the corners no one can see what I'm writing and I can see everyone. Tabatha said something to Lambo's wife—they were looking at me. Tabatha didn't even say goodbye. Lambo's is just a little place on the corner, in the Tenderloin somewhere, I think I'm on Geary or O'Farrell maybe Turk Street.... Does Monroe love me?

What time is it? I can't see that man's watch. Maybe it's 3:00 or 6:15 or 12:15 or 8:45. It looks like 6:15.

I'll just sit here and draw a picture for a minute.

FIVE MINUTES LATER

Lambo's wife brought me a hamburger wrapped in yellow paper with foil on one side. And some fries in a greasy red plastic basket lined with that same yellow paper-foil. And a vanilla shake. I looked at her, up at her, as she stood next to my little table with the red plastic laminate on top.

Some drawings from my notebook.

"I don't have any money," I said. She has huge boobs and a stained white apron tied tight around her chest, beneath her boobs. I think the apron helps hold the boobs in place.

"Tabatha paid for it. You know her pretty good?"

"I don't know."

SOME OTHER DAY

I guess I ran away because I've been gone for four or six days. I'm not sure but I think I could figure it out if I had a calendar.

I'm at Richie's house now. There's a lot of guys I know living here—Brandy and Randy and Tommy. Richie said an old queen pays the rent and the boys have to hustle for him. Richie said I could stay here for a while. He said I have to stay here until I come down. But it feels weird since I'm the only girl. I don't know if the others want me here. Richie was mad at me because he told me again and again that Tabatha was no good. I bet Chuck will be mad at me too.

Richie went out to pull a trick.

I still have all the meth Tabatha gave me. And I don't remember when I got it but there's $25.00 in my pocket.

Dear Diary,

They found out where I was. I told my mother I would not go home. She was crying. Monroe said I could stay at his house if my mom wanted me to. But I went home anyway. I felt so fucking sick. I took three Valiums an hour ago, and now I feel a lot better.

They all thought I ran away—but I hadn't intended to—things just ended up seeming I had. This is what happened:

I went down to Polk with Kimmie on Saturday and we ran into Tabatha at Nito Burrito. She singled me out as usual. She gave me two Quaaludes and said take them, but don't let Kimmie see, I don't have any for her. I drank them with coffee and she said you know I really dig you honey. That's how she talks, like a tough guy trying to pick you up, but if a guy spoke to me that way I'd be like, forget it, baby. She kissed me a little. She said let's go have some fun, honey. I said ok.

We went to crash for a while and get more 'ludes at her friend's house on Franklin near Market. We went up two flights of stairs in this pretty beaten-up place and Tabatha's friend Arthur, this black guy, opened the door and we went in. His brother was there, too. They were watching color TV. It was just one room, with two beds and some chairs and a kitchen table and a tv. We sat around and they gave us Southern Comfort and ice with half-and-half, really sweet, and they had loads of 'ludes, have another, baby, said one guy. Sure. Tabatha had to leave for a bit but she said she'd be right back. I watched tv with the guys. They were both quiet and seemed nice. We saw *Hee Haw*, and then *The Jeffersons*. I was so tired; I lay down on the bed I fell asleep listening to the TV and to Arthur and his brother laughing at the show.

I woke up a while later and some of my clothes were off and I was tucked under the covers. Arthur said they tried to make me comfortable. Tabatha had come back and left again, he said, because I was sleeping. He made me a grilled cheese sandwich with tomatoes. It was the best thing I ever had, melted in my mouth. I didn't have any idea how long I was asleep but I still felt tingly from the Quaaludes, pretty good cuddled in the covers with that sandwich. By then we were watching the news.

Tabatha came back again and she was really in a hurry. She told me to get my clothes on quick, because we were going to go get high.

He made me a grilled cheese sandwich with tomatoes.

We left and Arthur gave me a piece of paper with his address. He said I could come by any time I wanted. And he stuck something in Tabatha's pocket, like they thought I couldn't see. As soon as he shut the door and we were down the stairs, Tabatha shook a bottle of 'ludes that was almost full. I said, "Wow! He just gave it to you? He's pretty nice."

She said, tough as usual, "Yeah, you think so? Don't you know what they did? They gave me these 'cause I let them fuck you."

I wasn't upset because I didn't believe her. I know if they had fucked me, I would have woken up. She said, "No way, you passed out." I still didn't believe her because I had my period and I had a Tampax in and they couldn't have fucked me. She said they took it out and threw it in the trash. She said I could check for myself. She said she was there while they fucked me. She said she was watching for a while. "Your eyes were open," she said, "weren't you awake? I thought you might be awake, you looked like you were having fun."

I still didn't believe her but I was confused.

We went to Hippie David's in the Tenderloin on O'Farrell Street. He lives in the basement of The Crystal Ball Apartments. It was something like crystal ball, Tabatha called it crystal ball, she said let's go look in David's crystal ball and find the emerald city but it was spelled different... Crystobal?

Kristobahl? I can remember seeing the sign but I can't remember what was wrong with the spelling....

It was really dark in David's apartment and he was tall and thin and had long brown hair in a ponytail, and no shirt on.

Tabatha said, "C'mon, we're going to shoot."

I said, "No, I don't want to shoot."

"You wanna wake up, don't you? This is speed. This is crystal meth! Crystal ball, crystal meth!"

And David sat at the table and there was a box of Chex and I was startled that he ate normal food because he looked cold and white and damp like an albino salamander under a rock in a cave. He rolled his eyes and looked impatient and he started tying off his arm and then he said, "Come on, Tabatha, just let her drink it." There were cockroaches on the wall.

"Yeah," I said, "I wanna drink it."

David dumped some white powder in a plastic cup and poured some Coke over it and I drank it. Then they shot up. I never saw people shoot up before—the blood sucks back into the needle and mixes with the drugs and then you shoot it back in. It was like they were fucking themselves.

David did himself and then he did Tabatha. About a half a minute after he did her, she started staring at me and she looked mad. She grabbed my arm and she called me a stupid bitch and she yelled and she said, "You're gonna try it just once. You'll see, it's much better this way."

I didn't want to fight. I was afraid of her. I had never seen that mean side of her before so I let her do it and you should have felt it. It was a feeling that just lifted me out of the chair—it was a rush, it made my arms fly up and my heart was beating and I could feel the blood buzzing in my body and my hair stood on end.

She walked me over to the couch and I lay down. She took my clothes off. I just couldn't move, I was just feeling it. David came over and took his clothes off and started touching me and Tabatha was standing there and she kept saying, "It feels really really good when you're high." And it did feel good to be touched. David was feeling me all over but he couldn't get it up. Tabatha was standing there directing me, saying touch him, you have to play with him don't you fucking know how to do it? But it just wouldn't get hard. I felt bad and I asked Tabatha if it was my fault. She was at the table smoking a cigarette. "No, baby," she said, "you're beautiful."

I went to the bathroom because David was going to drive us somewhere. I looked at my body in the mirror and I did look beautiful, thin and white as a ghost.

I checked but I didn't have the Tampax inside and I kept trying to remember if I took it out myself or not, because I just didn't believe Tabatha. But I couldn't remember, and I started getting kind of paranoid.

And then, all the rest, I don't remember. I can't remember leaving the apartment.

As I figure it, there are two whole days I can't remember at all.

I remember when Tabatha dropped me off at Lambo's, but that was two days after we were at David's.

FRIDAY, DECEMBER 24

My mom had a tense phone conference with the principal. He says I can't come back to Lick-Wilmerding after Christmas vacation. They gave my mom the name of some school for drop-outs that I can go to. She is so mad at me but I don't give a care. She thinks that Dr. Wollenberg and Monroe share most of the blame.

I figured out if I take one Valium soon after I get up, then another one every few hours, I feel ok. Otherwise I feel really shitty.

Mom's also mad because she heard all about Tabatha and now she thinks I'm a lesbian and she says it disgusts her. She says lesbians are really sick because they just want to be men.

LATER

My mom asked to see my arms and I ran out of the room pretending to freak out. I tried to make it look like a joke. Like she's a fool to think I would shoot up. I think she's forgotten.

There are bruises all over me. I can hardly bend my arm at the elbow and my hand really hurts and is swollen from skin-popping.

CHRISTMAS

I have a horribly painful boil on my stomach. I noticed it yesterday when it was very small. When I woke up this morning, it was huge and red and hot. There are a few more starting on my legs. They really hurt. I had to go to the emergency room because doctors don't have office hours on Christmas. I was lying on a steel table wrapped in a white paper sheet looking at the ceiling for a half an hour while Mom sat next to me in an orange plastic chair and read Redbook. Gretel was home making a Christmas cake. The doctor gave me a shot and wrote a prescription for some antibiotics. She said I got a bad infection from shooting up. And I lost ten pounds and I didn't even know it. She said what I was doing was very dangerous and it's time to stop.

Mom was crying to the doctor that she has no idea what goes on and what I'm up to and that she thought I was shooting up but I lied to her.

I have a horribly painful boil on my stomach.

We wish you a Merry Christmas we wish you a Merry Christmas we wish you a Merry Christmas

I got clothes and books and records. David Bowie Pink Floyd Donna Summer.

Drinking some plum wine now. I'm very drunk. Cheers. I gave everyone candy because I only had time to go to the store around the corner. But I wrapped it up!

SUNDAY, DECEMBER 26

Monroe is here and I feel afraid of him. I am staying overnight at his house and I don't think he really wants me to... I said I'm not staying with my fucking mother, no way, so she told Monroe he had to let me stay there. She said I'm his problem now.

I'm in my room and I can hear him talking with my mother—she asked him to drive me to the drugstore and I overheard him saying that he was insulted that she would ask him to do that.... He probably hates how I look.

I'm wearing my new flat shoes and I probably look different. He's probably the type of man who hates that kind of change.

Oh my God, Monroe just said to my mother that he's mad because he was planning to party it up with some pals and he thought I was coming tomorrow night and that's why he's so mad. Do you understand—I'm overhearing all this so I know it's the unadulterated truth and no lie—he'd never tell me anything like that because he loves to mask the truth.

I think perhaps that I'll have to get drunk or something. I don't know where I can go. I'm sick and infected and full of hate, but I'll try to act like it doesn't faze me... then I'll slam it to him and tell him I heard him

———

I took more Valiums and I told them I'm just staying in my room, not going to Monroe's. I don't feel well. Monroe went to the pharmacy.

Gretel is really upset. I don't know how much she knows. She stays in her room most of the time. She came into my room earlier and said, "I'm very disappointed with your behavior, young lady." She wrote me a note inviting me to watch tv in her room. Maybe I'll go there in a little while.

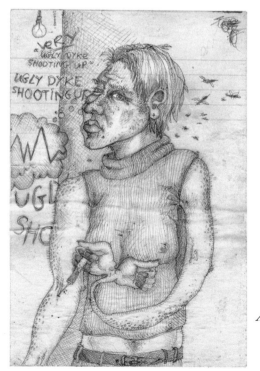

*A drawing I drew at
Richie's house.*

Dear Diary,

Today we had a very special dinner. We had scrapple and scrambled eggs—Pop-pop sent the scrapple fresh from Philadelphia in a freezer pack. Scrapple is my absolute favoritest thing to eat. I'll have to try and save some for Kimmie.

Andrea was here. She said I look great. Compared to what?

The boils started to get smaller but now they're itching. My arm still feels fucked up.

Mom lets me have wine now. She says anything to calm me down and keep me from taking drugs.

WEDNESDAY, JANUARY 5

The Lovely Vacation is Over!

I started the new school. The Independent Learning School. I need to be there until 3:00, but if your attendance is perfect for two weeks, you become a "floater" and can leave at 12:00 if your work is done. There is no homework. There are only about fifty students, and many of them are hyperactive mangy-looking little sixth-graders, and others are more my age, stoned skateboarder types, but also mangy-looking. I didn't see anyone to be friends with.

WEDNESDAY, JANUARY 12

I had perfect attendance at school for one week. If I make it 'til Friday I get a star next to my name on the wall chart.

THURSDAY, JANUARY 13

Wollenberg made me go take a test at an office near Stonestown to see if the drugs had damaged my brain. It was amusing. I think my brain does seem a little cloudy. I can't remember some things.

Sometimes I really don't know why or what I'm doing. It's become a conscious consideration—I'm tempted to get in contact with Hippie David and ask how much his speed is. If he knows I want it maybe he'll give Kimmie and me some for free. I'm kind of scared, though. There's cockroaches in his apartment and I'm a little afraid of needles. And he might expect us to make it with him. If he can.

Maybe I'm a speed freak.

Oh, Diary, you can't believe how bad I've been. I haven't been honest with you or myself or my psychiatrist or anyone else. In fact, when I utter the words that are the truth, they seem strange and don't melt into me. The truth seems like a light joke because everything is tied together by a short school day and no homework.

I love Polk Street. I love drugs I love disco music I love fags and dykes and coffee and cigarettes.

And I must have said it before, but I've got to tell myself again and again... I love drugs. I love speed. I love snorting it, shooting it, drinking it, popping it—crank, crystal meth, white crosses, Dexedrine, anything.

I went home sick from school. I had cramps. I think I look pretty good today, kind of loose and dark and sexy. I just got high from two roaches (small ones!). It must have been good dope—I'm pretty wasted. I want to practice getting high a lot so I can learn to maintain. I'm listening to Pink Floyd.

I think I'm a beautiful, complex person. I don't want myself to die, but then sometimes I don't care if I do, and sometimes I am overpowered by a wish that I would. It's so easy to really have fun fun fun when you're able to say that you don't care.

On Polk at night, all the people walk up the street and down again, from Geary to California, and back again. It makes me laugh to think about it, but it's fun if you know everyone, which I almost do. It seems like more people know me than I know. A lot of times, they come up to me and say, "Hi, Minnie," and I'll say, "oh, hi," even though I don't recognize them!

I know when I see Tabatha, she'll be as cold as the fucking North Pole, but still I just can't wait. I know everybody's been telling her to stay away from me, and I know I should be mad at her, but she fascinates me so and I know I could never get close to her anyway. I really just love watching her and what she does.

Do you think I'll be alive when I'm thirty?

I hope Kimmie comes here tonight so we can go out and have fun. Now, where is there to go in San Francisco on a rainy Tuesday night?

1. Polk St.
2. Have a party down at Julius Kahn Park under the bushes behind the chain-link fence—who to invite?
    a. Some fags
    b. Chuck
    c. Anyone else can come too
3. We can go to someone's house if their parents aren't home.
4. We can go to a bar and get drunk, if they serve us.
5. We can get drunk anyplace else cheaper.
6. We can go to the movies.
7. We can go to Polk and look for drugs.
8. We can get a ride down to Baker Beach and sleep there.
9. We can look at the lesbian bar on Geary and get scared.
10. We can find a party.

SUNDAY, JANUARY 23

why why why
why why why
never ever never
ever never ever again.
How can I

Why is Tabatha so appealing to me? She's such a fox, and everything about her is sexy. She does things like lean me against a wall and push her pelvis into mine when she kisses me she tells me I'm beautiful she pushes her thigh between my legs she pushes she pushes me the love I feel for her is like the love I feel for myself, mixed with hatred and violence.

MONDAY, JANUARY 24

Tonight I was kissing Tabatha at a party on Upper Market and some guy who's always flirting with me saw us. I think he went to Lick-Wilmerding, I can't even remember how I know him. When I noticed him staring, I laughed and told him I liked girls—and boys, I added, but he didn't smile and wouldn't even look at me after that.

But at the next party that night, in an apartment above the active part of Castro Street, Tabatha first ignored me then got more obviously irritated and told me to get lost and quit bugging her. She obviously wanted to hang out with another girl she saw there, Tara, who Kimmie said is a spoiled little bitch. She's really skinny and pretty and I think she's only fourteen. Kimmie knows her brother from school in South San Francisco.

TUESDAY, JANUARY 25

Physical fight with Tabatha last night.

Doc is a veteran and he doesn't have any legs. He accused me of being a tease and a whore.

I am back in his room at the Donnelly Hotel. I just wanted to see if Tabatha was still alive. Tabatha chose Tara over me. They are asleep now. We're listening to them snore. Tabatha can sleep anywhere, anytime. But you better watch out if you wake her up. It's like disturbing a sleeping animal … she wakes up kicking and scratching, as if you were trying to kill her.

We were all in his room last night shooting whatever Doc had. Doc wanted to get turned on so Tabatha started making out with Tara on a bare mattress on the floor and it pissed me off so I kicked her. We got into a real fight. She's strong but I know I beat the fucking shit out of her. She bit my arm until it bled but I got my thighs around her middle, from the back so she couldn't grab me with her hands and I pulled her hair and yanked back her head and bit her shoulder down to the bone. I tasted her blood in my mouth. Then I jumped up and kicked her as many times as I could before she could get up. Then I spit at her. Spit her own blood back at her.

Little Tara was crying, boo hoo, boo hoo.

I spent the night with a horny compassionate black man down the hall. After the fight I knocked on his door and I asked if I could sleep there. He said I could. I curled up in his bed with my clothes on. He kept pushing his dick up against my butt but I ignored him and he didn't make me have sex with him or anything. I would have puked if he had.

I am still very high and injured. I have a swollen hand from shooting up and terrible ugly bruises on my arm. I know I should go home. I have such fatigued pain. I spewed out some foul imprecations last night—don't ask if they were returned. My arm hurts.

She's strong but I know I beat the fucking shit out of her.

Chuck will be so pissed at me. He said if I wanted to shoot so bad I could come to him, if I were that desperate. He is disgusted that I still try to run with Tabatha.

When I was throwing up outside the window in Doc's room last night Tabatha slammed it down on my back ouch.

FRIDAY, JANUARY 28

Dear Diary,

I have made a personal resolution never to take drugs again. I will even call Kimmie and tell her that I don't want to go to Rocky Horror. It's an unhealthy atmosphere. I'm too tempted to get high and hang out and run away. I don't know if I can straighten myself out. I still have a little envelope of meth in my purse and I don't want to throw it away. I'll give it to someone.

SATURDAY, JANUARY 29

I have dreams about Tabatha. I dream that she sees me at The Strand one Saturday night and she strides up to me and mutters something unintelligible and tilts her head slightly towards her chest and looks at me with her huge cat eyes and slugs me in the gut.

I am constantly in a state of limbo between two worlds maybe three and I can't wait to get drunk on Saturday night. But I have been going to school, almost every day. I'm a floater, so I'm there just until 12:00. It's weird; I don't have anything to do after that. I could go home, but it's depressing. If I go to Polk Street that early, no one I know is out yet.

MONDAY, JANUARY 31

My mom saw "vibrator" on the invoice from Dr. Wollenberg and she wanted to know what the hell he gave me that for. I said, "I don't know, he just did."

Later, when I was in my room with the door closed, she knocked, and I said "just a minute!" because I was getting my nightgown on.

"I know what you're doing in there," she said.

"Fuck you," I said. "I'm changing my clothes, as if it's any of your business."

"I know what you're doing in there."

LATER

I got a letter from Pascal.

Dear Minnie,

It was wonderful to hear those high octaves of yours last night. Your voice—in spite of your sleepiness—always rises a little with excitement. It is a characteristic of you. And it is a welcoming like no other to a wicked stepfather like me. I do miss you.

This weekend in New York was an afterthought. I had planned the weekend in Scotland. Recovery from a heavy cold and general ennui with the thought of sharing my brother's dull existence made me rearrange travel plans.

They now go like this: London on Monday and Tuesday; Frankfurt from Wednesday until the following Wednesday, a week, you'll note; back to London a day or two then home to New York. The main objective of the trip is the Frankfurt Book Fair. Strange thing is that all my colleagues are VPs or Ps or Chairmen: all chiefs. I am the Indian.

I heard from your mother that you seemed to be starting to apply yourself at school. Does school seem more exciting now that you are in the second semester of your junior year? What subjects are you working on? What is happening to your mind? Boys? Don't forget that girls who start early in that arena sometimes finish in the bottom half. Work on your brain and find a brainy man.

Now there I go again giving you gratuitous advice, and you so grown up. It is just fatherly advice. But, lil' Min, I do meet so many women who have been slaves to their inferiors in the man's world. I hope I raised you, of all the rest, to respect that pretty mind of yours. Naturally I wonder whose influence on you and Gretel was greatest: Mom's or mine. I suppose it was a pastiche of both. Now you're you.

Working for a large corporation has its drawbacks. For one thing it creates bureaucrats. Very little gets done between secretary and Vice President. Very frustrating. However, there are advantages, obvious ones, which balance the equation. I do feel stimulated to do things I put on the side when I was at F— in California. Almost all the people around me have written books. Yesterday I had lunch with EH—, editor-in-chief of—. I am a senior editor with that magazine. She has written several books. The other morning, another of my colleagues was on "Good Morning America" to plug hers. I tell you, it is really a stimulating environment. Still not everyone would want that, I guess. Why don't you write a story?

Well, sweetheart, I must get on with the day's activities.

Love you. Pascal.

SATURDAY, FEBRUARY 5

I've never known what it's like to have someone really love me, which is what I've always wanted, I think, someone to love me no matter what and let me know it, someone I could love.... I wish I knew how to accept love and give love freely.

I still love Tabatha somehow. I know she's bad but I still want her. I know Kimmie loves me. And I love her. I know she needs me, and I need her. But I want to get close to someone physically, too—and I don't think that Kimmie and I would ever make love.

You know, I've been thinking about Pascal. He's said that there will always be a place for me with him, and that he will always offer me "domicile."

Maybe I could move to New York and live with him and finish high school there.

I know my mother hasn't told him everything that's going on here. She's ashamed. She's afraid someone will think it's her fault. I want to tell him everything and see if he'll take me in. I really think I'm ready to change.

Elizabeth's coming up here next weekend. She wants to see how I'm doing. She said she's going to bring the pictures she took of New York and Pascal's neighborhood. I'll ask her what she thinks about my idea.

It's been so long since I've stayed up late, alone, puttering around in my room, working. It feels good. It makes me remember that I am alone. Alone, as an individual. But the more I do, the more I have to share with others.

WEDNESDAY, FEBRUARY 9

I felt sort of sick this morning, so I didn't go to school.

Actually, I just didn't want to go.

I am on the bus now. The 3 Jackson heading towards home. Dr. Wollenberg gave me a note to excuse my absence from school today. He lied for me. My sense of responsibility to myself is reinforced now, because I must be responsible to him, too, because he cared enough to bail me out. He invested his trust in me. He thinks I am worth risking his integrity because he believes I can make something of myself.

He says I have to stop taking drugs. He told me that the test he gave me showed that my iq had fallen ten points compared to test results from school a year ago. He said that typically, the iq would bounce back up two to six months after a person stopped taking drugs. He said that I was extremely bright and shouldn't compromise my intelligence.

Truthfully, he sometimes makes me feel creepy. Like I'm a guinea pig.

I told him I think I like girls better than men and he said he didn't believe it. He said, "Close your eyes, and imagine an erect penis." Then he asked me if I felt "aroused." I could not believe he asked me that and I just giggled like an idiot and said I wasn't going to tell him.

I asked him what he thought of the possibility of me going to live with Pascal next year. He said he could think of advantages and disadvantages. He said that we'd talk more about it.

I stayed in bed all day.

Have I been good?

I think I've been doing pretty well lately, trying to stay on track, trying to go to school and to do things that are good for me instead of fucking up.

Very good.

But things are really very bad, much worse than I imagined, and looking back, I should have known all along.

Elizabeth came, and brought all her pictures. Pascal's apartment looked pretty posh. There were a few pictures of people from Castilleja. Some pictures of Sarah Lawrence.

She said that Pascal's doorman took the last picture, in front of his building. Pascal had his arm around Elizabeth, like a Dad. They were smiling. Of course I felt a twinge of jealousy. I thought he looked proud to be with her. She's a precocious young woman. She'll be seventeen when she starts college.

We're sitting there, on my bed, looking at this picture, and she starts bawling. "I'm sorry! I'm sorry!" Tears streaming, nose running. I had no idea what was wrong with her. The only thing I could think of was that she was sorry for being such a smart little straight-a student because I'm such a fuck-up.

But that was not the reason she was sorry.

She slept with Pascal on that trip back east. She didn't tell me before because she knew it would freak me out.

She slept with him again when she was back in California over Christmas. He was in LA for business, I guess. How could he do it?

Elizabeth is pretty fucked up. I think she's in love with Pascal or something. We know how that goes.... She's gone now.

I stayed in bed all day. I'm in bed now. I don't want to get out of bed.

That's why Pascal was always so suspicious of Monroe. Because he was thinking about fucking Elizabeth.

Takes one to know one.

I stole a whole bottle of Valiums from my mother. She'll never notice. She has prescriptions from three different doctors.

Wollenberg says he's not surprised about Pascal.

My mom wasn't surprised about Pascal either. She said that when they lived in Philadelphia and he was a calculus professor, he was giving private lessons to a high school girl from Shipley. She was sixteen or seventeen. He was fucking her. That's just how he is. Oh.

Why am I the only one who is surprised? Did everyone know about him and just not tell me? I hate them all, including Monroe. I feel so betrayed by everyone. Elizabeth too.

I hate Pascal. I'm glad I saved all his letters. I can look at them with new eyes now, and clearly see him for the bullshit artist that he is. One that seduces you with false concern as he makes you believe he's accepted you in his pretentious exclusive inner circle. He's just like Monroe but more evil because he's smarter and understands his own intent. He's a liar through and through and I thought he loved me like a father.

Man, I love the jukebox here. I need a Tampax.

I've never seen the inside of a barroom,
Or listened to a jukebox all night long,
But I see these are the things that bring you pleasure,
So I'm going to make some changes in our home.
I've heard it said if you can't beat 'em, join 'em,
So if that's the way you've wanted me to be,
I'll buy some brand new clothes and dress up fancy,
From now on you're gonna see a different me
Because your good girl's gonna go bad,
She's gonna be the swinginest swinger you ever had, blahhh ...
　　　　　—Tammy Wynette

Oh god what to write I'm tired.

Epilogue

In which I prevail
for a moment
over the feelings
which have bound me
and come to realize
that no matter how precariously
close to the end it may feel,
my life has really only just begun.

———

This diary is almost full. The binder rings can barely hold another few pages but I just didn't get a new diary binder yet. Maybe I'll go downtown to Patrick's...they probably have a nice serious-looking black binder with heavy-duty rings that won't burst open. That's what I want. I want to get a good one.

I haven't been writing at all because I've been waiting to start a new diary. A brand-new diary is like a brand-new life, and I'm ready to leave this one behind me. But since I don't have a new binder, it's just too bad: I'll have to tack a few pages onto my old life.

So... what's new???

I haven't even smoked pot in nearly a month.

Mom had a big dinner party so everyone could meet her new boyfriend, B—, the other cartoonist in Crumb's band. He is an unusually nice guy and I hope my mother stays with him for a while. He plays the steel guitar and the saw (with a violin bow)! Most of the guys in the band live out in the country near Sacramento. We've been up there a few times already—it's really hot there and B— lives in an old farmhouse in the middle of an almond orchard. One afternoon we sat on the porch drinking beer in the afternoon while B— and his friend tried to pick off squirrels with their shotguns. They were pissed that the squirrels were always after the nuts, even though the guys don't even own the nuts or the orchard, they only rent the house. I was kind of upset, although I didn't show it. I was praying that they wouldn't kill any squirrels and they didn't! They missed every shot.

In the morning we wanted to make pancakes with fresh eggs that the hen laid but when my Mom picked up an egg to add to the batter and tapped it on the side of the bowl, it exploded! It was green inside and smelled like death and ruined the batter and stank up the whole house.

B—'s roomate took me and Gretel to some old general store on a candy expedition later that day in his pick-up truck. All three of us spent $5.00 apiece on all sorts of penny candy and other stuff—Now 'n Laters, wax lips, B-B Bats.

I like this song the band sings:

> *Quit my job*
> *And spent three months in bed*
> *Thought I'd take up fine-art painting instead*
> *Bought myself some canvas and three bottles of paint*
> *Five minutes' work is going to make me a saint*

> refrain
> *Baby I'm a fine artiste*
> *And baby I deserve to be kissed*

I haven't seen Monroe at all. Mom finally agreed not to invite him over here, at least for a month or so. She still sees him, though. It's like they're still best friends or something. She doesn't understand why I don't want him around. It pisses me off in a way. She said that he's getting his real estate license renewed because he might want to move back East. He's going to give the Athletic Dietary Nutritional Supplement business another six months to turn a profit. If it doesn't pan out, he's going to cut his losses and sell it. I hope he moves soon.

Pascal called a couple times and I hung up on him.

School is going well. I've been tutoring a few of the little kids in French. Even though I can't remember any grammar it doesn't matter because they're just learning beginning words and things like "Je m'appelle Warren," and "Ou est le chien," and such.

I'm still seeing Dr. Wollenberg and he thinks even though I'm such a fuck-up I'll get into some kind of college because my test scores are good. And I have one more year to try to get some good grades....

Gretel is going to University High School for next year. It's really a hard school to get accepted to.

I haven't seen Kimmie or Tabatha or Polk Street or even had sex all this time. It feels strange, being such a hermit but that's what I want at the moment. I'm going to see Chuck tomorrow, though, because he called to see how I was doing. He said he was really worried about me after all that Tabatha shit. He was glad that I wasn't doing any drugs and he says he's been clean for two weeks.

We are planning to take a long walk out to the beach.

I got high one last time yesterday. I know it was the last time—I feel different.... I had a bag of meth that I had saved, and Chuck and I decided to do it.
Anyway, we didn't shoot it, we just snorted some and mixed the rest in a soda,
and now it's long gone.

It was such a beautiful day down by the beach, and I was itching to
draw or write... we got the idea to write a bunch of poems and try to sell
them to the tourists in front of the Cliff House, so we spent about an hour
writing and then we situated ourselves on a wall by the totem pole and we
sold a few for fifty cents each... an old lady bought one from each of us and
seemed quite worried about what we were doing... a gay guy bought one
from Chuck and gave him his phone number.

My best poem
> I fucked the Chinaman
> I fucked the old man
> I fucked the small black-eyed Chicano
> And the nigger fucked me.
>
> I fucked the White man sometimes
> And sometimes he fucked me
> The Black man was always watching
> But him I could not see.
>
> I saw the vomit on Polk Street
> Young boys arm in arm
> Their eyes wide and rolling
> Hands in each other's pockets
> Laughing hysterically at the vomit.

A poem by Chuck
> <u>Streets</u>
> I ran away from home
> I went to the streets
> I was all alone,
> I hung around with creeps.
> Now I'm writing a poem
> I'm turning into a freak
> I am very cheap.

At one point Chuck jumped the wall and went down to the beach to pee so I was alone for a minute. I sat there, pleasantly speeding and enjoying the warm sun, and I looked up and who do I see in the distance but Monroe, jogging down the Great Highway towards me, as yet ignorant of my presence. It was funny to see him like that, in public, as if he were just another stranger, just some middle-aged guy doing his heavy-footed jog, clumsily weaving through the blur of tourists in front of the Cliff House, looking somewhat self-conscious in his new bright blue running shorts. He probably thought they were darker, more navy blue, when he bought them.

For that first moment I saw him, before I even thought about it, my heart leapt to my throat and I struggled between yearning and nausea. Chuck returned just about the time Monroe reached our spot, still oblivious to me. I had to practically trip him to get him to stop. He seemed quite surprised. He and Chuck had never met before, so I stood up and introduced them.

"Chuck's the guy I got the acid from—you remember, when you had that bad trip?" I said this knowing that it was one of the many things Monroe would rather forget.

"Oh yeah. Sure. Interesting." He looked at Chuck as though he were a street person, as if he were dirty or something. I think street people scare Monroe.

Monroe was jogging in place so Chuck and I started doing it too, just for fun.

Monroe was jogging in place.

"I'm better than you, you son-of-a-bitch."

We convinced Monroe to buy a poem but he didn't have any money in his new jogging shorts. He promised to get it to me next time he sees my Mom, and shook my hand to seal the deal. I looked up at his blonde face, his eyes squinting nervously in the sun, and I felt that he wanted to get away from us as soon as possible.

I suddenly recalled something Pascal taught me years ago. I looked Monroe in the eye as I shook his hand firmly, and I thought to myself,

"I'm better than you, you son-of-a-bitch."

With this thought in my head, it was easy to forget the love I once felt for him and I felt unusually powerful and in control of the situation, despite the fact that I was somewhat high, and that Monroe is a foot taller than me and more than twice my age. It was exhilarating. After Monroe left, I told Chuck about it, and he's going to try it out for himself next time he sees his sister-in-law.

The poem I sold to Monroe ($.75) was one of the last ones I had, and not the best. It was one I wrote in fourth grade, and I know it by heart,

> Mabel Rushmore, very trite
> Crosses at a yellow light.
> The birds, they twitter,
> A car has hit her!

> I hope he enjoys it.

God Bless Us All.

Signing off forever, dear Diary...

Minnie Goetze

THE END

Notes

Music/Poems/Spoken word recordings

PAGE ix: by Abby Hutchinson, singer and suffragist, from "Kind Words Can Never Die" (circa 1880), as published in *The Book of a Thousand Songs*, edited by Albert E. Weir, World Syndicate Co., New York, 1918.

PAGES 70 AND 142: poem by Akazome Emon (circa 1020), translated by William N. Porter in *A Hundred Verses from Old Japan*, The Clarendon Press, 1909.

PAGES 89-92: from "The Strangest Secret and the Mind of Man," 1972 audiotape, recorded by Earl Nightingale, Nightingale-Conant Corporation. For more information on the work of Earl Nightingale, call 800-525-9000, or go to www.nightingale.com. Used by permission.

PAGE 109: lines from the song "White Punks on Dope," as performed by The Tubes on the album *The Tubes*. © 1975: Evans, Spooner, Steen. Bern Doubt Music, Pseudo Songs, Irving Music, 1975. Used by permission.

PAGE 137: lines from the song "Freight Train" by Elizabeth Cotten. Permission in process at time of printing.

PAGE 174: lines from the song "Baby Boy," performed by the character Loretta (Mary Kay Place) on the show *Mary Hartman Mary Hartman*. Words and music © 1975: Mary Kay Place. Used by permission.

• ORIGINAL DIARIES *and* PHOTOS •

On the next several pages, you will find various items related to the creation
of this book: drawings; photographs from the mid-1970s of the author and
her sister, her cat Domino, and the building they all lived in (middle flat);
and a few original pages from her diary binder.

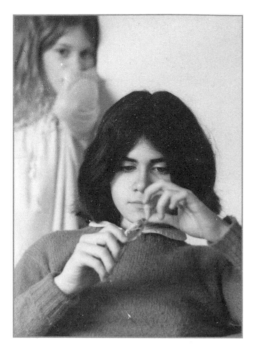

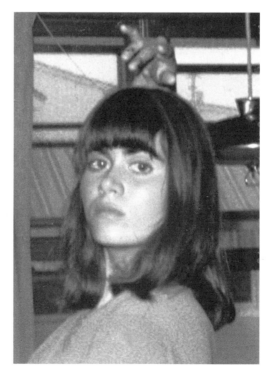

      I was terribly upset. I had cleaned the kitchen thouroughly
and my mother had promised that I could go with Mc——and her to
the airport. But Mc—— said no,that I couldn't go. I don't
know why. It all is af little importance. Anyway,I went into my
room and cryed desparately for a short while then stiffened my
upper lip and wiped away my tears and snuck a beer into my purse
(I was already ineibriated with the two glasses of wine I had had
at dinner) then I told everyome I was going to visit Trische ——
——. Instead,I took a 55 on down to Chinatown.I was going to get
off at Polk,but something stopped me. It was lucky that I got off
where I did. Because I met a man,George ——,an old man,about 70,
who was once a gardener in Golden Gate Park. We talked for a long
while,and walked through Chinatown....he poured out his philos-
ophies of life to me,and made me more aware of my possibilities as
a person,and made me realize that a person is self made,that one
may exceot or reject any influences into of from his personality.
He tought me that I had to grow and learn my aspirations,realiz-
ing that I can never reach perfection on the earth but that I should
try to be humble and loving and understanding and divinely sweet
and of good will because I had potential as a good happy and friendly
person because I was sensitibe He said women were God's most
perfect creation because they are|more heart than mind and less
cold and more understanding and they have intuition which is a
godly type of understanding He told me that it was a sin to live
a usless empty life and that I should do what I can with what I've
got and not be pretentious and that I should stay pure and bright
and innocent in my own mind and the ultimate goal of a marriage
should be to bear childrea and if someone dosen't plan to gét/ﬁ
have children they shouldn't marry unless they're old and it's
more for companionship anyway. that man actually thought I was
pure and innocent he kept telling me so he said I should keep my
angel eyes everyone has bad thoughts heﬀ said it's only human
there are very few bad women he saﬁd.There are wrong women,but
very few bad women. There are bad men though,just as much as there
are wrong men. But there are very few bad women.
      I'm going to invite him to dinner one night when my mother gets
back from Las Vegas. She's at a trial for a robbery.Smoe of her
jewelery was stolen in a hotel in las vegas a few months ago.
      A man shoﬁld strive to be honest and to live simply and humbly.
Then is he closet to God. Complications ﬁﬁﬁ such as wild night
life and the accquition of material goods really doesn't not make
one happieer. Man is meant to live simply What he has that makes
him different fromthe animals is understanding,.

As me said that you should remember that there is always someone
who loves you and cares for you as you are and will except you in
no holds barred....that is god. One can not expect to have such a
perfect relationship with any other human being it would be asking
too much...human beings are naturally selfish and aannot sacrifice
completely their pride and ego and give there entire heart and sooul
to another human being. Because they are only human.

It really hurts to admit it,but I think I have figured out
the way M____ thinks of me. He likes me very much as a friend like
my sister ____,or even a little more....but he also likes to go to
bed with me,and the two are not related. It's different for me though.
THe two aspects of our relationship mingle in my mind and though
he likes me just as much as I like him it's in a different way.
And that's why I always feel so desparate because I half expect
himto feel the same way I do.....but I souldn't expect anything.
I should just see thin gs the way they are....but /I am too often
blinded by trying to look at things as though they are about to
become any minute the way I hope they will.

M____ is a friend. But I need somebody to love love.

my mother is so sweet. She called and understands how
difficalt it is to be alone with my grandparents when there is no
 way out......she said she'd take me to the beach any and every
dsy I wanted to as soon as they left.   My only worriment is that
what if I ever getreally close to her and we talk about sex and eer-
ything else....then I'll want to tell her about M____I know and
if I don't I feel incompletely with her and kind of guilty especially
if she thinks she knows everything   but there are some
things you just can't tell   I know it would really hurt her. It
wpuld really kill her. She'd just think of M____and my relation
ship in relation to herself and she'd be hurt hurt hurt....it's
really a pity I wish I had someone Not gossipy and who cared about
me like her that I could talk to about it. That's exactly what I
need It's sad and kind ofunfair.

Some things are too complicated to type down on paper. You just
would not understand them even if they were described in the most me
ticulous detail. That is because there rarely is any detail. It is
quite difficult to bring these things into focus...even the most
powerful astronomical telescopes or the most modern electron microscopes used by man are worthless in the persual of..................
you know i don't quite know exactly what I mean..let's say....just
for sake of the story,that we're looking for...

did you know that it would be possible to go back in time like in
atime machine..if you could travel faster than the speed of light?
because,well,you know that you only can see things because light is
reflected off them. And light is constantly traveling. Some stars
I mean,all stars,are a number of light years away. Which means,well,
suppose a star was 6 light years away. That means that the light we
are seeing is six years old-the star is so far away that it took the
light from it six years to reach our eyes. This also means that the
star could disappear ƒø this minute,and we wouldn't know it for unti
l six years from now.
What I'm driving at...the light reflected off some dinosaur..that
is,the image of that dinosaur,is traveling through space right now
and has been for the past 50 million years. If we could ever travel
faster than the speed of light,which is the speed the dinosaur is
going at,we could catch up to it,and be,literally,behind in time.
Just as we see that hypothetical star as it was six years ago,peo
ple on a hypothetical planet,which,lets say,is also six light years
away,are seeing us,the planet earth,as it was six years ago.
This means that if they were,somehow in possesion of a super-powerful telescope that could see details on a planet as far away from th
em as earth would be,they would see _____; only 28 years ol
d,married to _____,and they'd see nixon as president and
uncle jimmy alive....and _____ would still have her hair lon
g...well,don' you see what I mean?   I think it's all very neat.

m_____ just wrestled me he squeezed me tight between his thigh
s and he wouldn't let go   I was very nice tonight so he was nice t
o me in return for a change. He said maybe he'd take me out Thursday
night if you know what I mean   well even if he doesn't it's the
thought that counts.
I've been very profilie Prolific??? in my writing today.
I mean that I've written alot

                Goodbye and Goodnight.
                    Love
                        Little Phoebe

September 18.

Dear Diary,

The only reason I'm writing is because I am not allowed to make any noise. My mother is asleep; m—— is napping on the couch; —— is quietly puttering around, and I am sitting peacefully upon my bed. It is only 3:55 in the afternoon.

3:56 On the surface my body feels very cold but my cheeks are flushed my blood is hot.

M—— last night said that he thought we should stop our physical relationship I said no I don't want to. We went to his apartment after the restaurant he said if we made love would it screw you up I said no I won't ever be jealous I won't he said I won't get involved. We made love he said yes it would be good if we could do this and not have it get complicated

The first time we made love I had my sweater on still + he had his shirt + his jacket + his socks

I got a post card from aline kominsky whom I wrote to and whom is also a comic artist who did Twisted Sisters + who lives with Robert Crumb——

List of Illustrations

Illustrations in Text

Comics

Acknowledgments for this Edition

There are many to whom I am indebted for helping bring this edition about. In particular, I'd like to thank Richard Grossinger and North Atlantic Books, Hillary Chute at the University of Chicago, Carl Greene, Kath Weider-Roos, and Kate West at the University of Michigan Stamps School of Art and Design, and my agent, Amy Williams.

Pipsqueak. You were
always by my side. We were
the very best of friends. See
you later, no?

Thank You.

Also by PHOEBE GLOECKNER

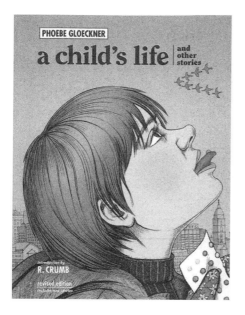

A collection of comic stories created from 1976-1998, with an introduction by R. Crumb.

"Phoebe Gloeckner's *A Child's Life and Other Stories* is as perfect a publishing project as we're likely to see this calendar year: it collects short stories, both new and previously-published, from a period of over 20 years; the stories are consistently interesting and some are downright excellent; and the experience of reading all of the work in one place creates an artistic whole greater than the sum of its parts."
—Tom Spurgeon, *The Comics Journal*

ISBN: 978-1-58394-028-0
$18.95, trade paper, 152 pages.
www.northatlanticbooks.com